*The American
Immigration Collection*

Immigration: Its Evils and Consequences

SAMUEL S. BUSEY
09935

Arno Press and The New York Times

NEW YORK 1969

IMMIGRATION:

ITS

EVILS AND CONSEQUENCES.

BY

SAMUEL C. BUSEY, M.D.

"We should become a little more Americanized."—JACKSON.

———◆———

NEW YORK:

DE WITT & DAVENPORT, PUBLISHERS,

160 AND 162 NASSAU STREET

W. H. TINSON, STEREOTYPER.   GEO. RUSSELL & CO., PRINTERS.   G. W. ALEXANDER, BINDER.

PREFACE.

THE object of this book is simply to present to the American people, in a convenient form, the "facts and figures" in relation to immigration. The author has studiously avoided hypotheses and conjectures, and relied solely and exclusively upon positive illustrations to demonstrate practically the evils and consequences of indiscriminate immigration; and the evidence employed to substantiate any one of the evils enumerated as flowing from immigration, is only such as is authoritative and indisputable. The census of 1850 constitutes the basis of all the tabular statements, and the conclusions deduced therefrom are only such as seemed to be clearly within the comprehension of every reflecting mind. It has been an especial aim of the author to avoid all mere partisan statements, and any comment upon any fact which was calculated to exaggerate the evil or give to it a coloring not justified by the data, and if in any instance he has erred it has been an error of judgment.

CONTENTS.

IMMIGRATION.

CHAPTER I.

INTRODUCTION.

THE repeal or amendment of the naturalization laws is one of the political questions now agitating the public mind, and it is important that all collateral questions or issues bearing, in any manner, upon this momentous question, should be fully and thoroughly investigated, discussed, and understood. The reasons, pro and con, should be fully and fairly set forth. It is the object of this work to show cause for a repeal of the existing laws, or the necessity of an amendment, which will extend the term of probation of aliens, and require them to reside long enough amongst us to clearly comprehend the workings of a popular government, and to understand and appreciate the laws and municipal regulations of the country. The machinery of the government is so intricate, yet so nicely adjusted, with its admirably arranged checks and balances, that, to fully comprehend its operation, it is not only necessary to study it theoretically, but to observe it in all its varied and multiform phases, and to experience, feel, and enjoy its blessings, its liberality, and its security, to become acquainted with the scope of its powers, their necessity, their source, their object, their action, and their effect.

The untutored alien, however honest and patriotic he may be, and however thoroughly imbued with the principles of civil and religious liberty, cannot acquaint himself with the complex machinery in the brief period required by the existing laws.

The circumstances under which he was reared, his education, his training, the associations of his youth, have impressed upon his mind the peculiarities of his race and of his country. He has inherited the customs and habits of his parents, learned their sympathies, and imbibed their prejudices and animosities. The associations of youth stamp their impress upon the character of the grown up man, and give bent to the mind. The endearments of the past cling around him in the future, and the ties of relationship and companionship cannot be severed.

Every nation possesses distinctive peculiarities, not only in reference to its habits, customs, dress, and manners, but also in morals, religion, language, and in politics; and these peculiarities, whether of the person or of the mind, of society or of the nature, are so uniform and well marked in all nations, that they have been regarded as tests. Language and dress are not the only characteristics of nations. The qualities of the mind and of the heart of different nations are as dissimilar as their language and dress. These distinctive features are essential to the well-being of mankind. Destroy them, and the nation will soon cease to exist. A nation's nationality consists in its distinctive characteristics; its government is constituted, and its laws are framed with national peculiarities, and as one nation becomes blended and commingled with another, its form of government and laws gradually change, its institutions give way, and others are established. This change may be gradual or not, beneficial or deleterious, as the circumstances of the case may be.

Every civilized country has its government, its laws, and its institutions. The citizens are trained up under the operation of those laws, and under the established institutions, and the effect and influence of such training upon the mind, the feelings and impulses, upon the nature and character are powerful and durable. The government is the political school of its citizens, wherein they are taught the justice of its laws, and the liberality and beneficence of its institutions, and these teachings form and give direction to all ideas of government, of laws, and of their effect and purpose.

In his "Notes on Virginia," speaking of the population of America, the author of the Declaration of Independence said :

"Here I will beg leave to propose a doubt. The present desire of America is to produce a rapid population, by as great importation of foreigners as possible. But is this founded in good policy? * * * * Are there no inconveniences to be thrown into the scale against the advantages expected from the multiplication of numbers, by the importation of foreigners? It is for the happiness of those united in society to harmonize, as much as possible, in matters which they must of necessity transact together. Civil government being the sole object of forming societies, its administration must be conducted by common consent. Every species of government has its specific principles. Ours, perhaps, are more peculiar than any other in the universe. It is a composition of the freest principles of the English constitution, with others, derived from natural right and reason. To these nothing can be more opposed than the maxims of absolute monarchies. Yet from such we expect the greatest number of emigrants. They will bring with them the principles of the governments they have imbibed in early youth; or if able to throw them off, it will be in exchange for an unbounded licentiousness, passing, as is usual, from one extreme to another. *It would be a miracle were they to stop precisely at the point of temperate liberty.* Their principles, with their language, they will transmit to their children. In proportion to their number they will share with us in the legislation. They will infuse into it their spirit, warp and bias its direction, and render it a heterogeneous, incoherent, distracted mass. I may appeal to experience, during the present contest, for a verification of those conjectures; but if they are not certain in event, are they not possible, are they not probable? Is it not safer to wait with patience for the attainment of population desired or expected? May not our government be more homogeneous, more peaceable, more durable?"

" Our government," said Jefferson, " is a composition of the freest principles of the English Constitution, with others, derived from natural right and reason." Should a government, thus constituted, be entrusted to the keeping of those who have neither enjoyed, nor who understand the principles, " of natural right and reason?" "They will," said Jefferson, "infuse into it their spirit, warp and bias its direction, and render it a heterogeneous, incoherent, distracted mass." Whence comes the immigrant? France is monarchical, Spain is despotic, Russia autocratic. Ireland is but a British dependency; and ours is a government of constitutional liberty, and of "natural right and reason," to "which nothing can be more opposed than the 'maxims of absolute monarchies.'" "It is for the happiness of those united in society to harmonize as much as possible, in matters which they must, of necessity, transact together. Civil government being the sole object of forming societies, its administration must be conducted by common consent." A government, to be lasting, durable, uniform in policy and its institutions, must be homogeneous. This is a political truism. A government, to be homogeneous, must preserve the homogeneity of its citizens, of its people, and the homogeneity of a people can only be preserved by the continuance or multiplication of its kind by generation or successive production, and there is not in nature any spontaneous generation, but all comes by propagation.

Immigration is then, inconsistent with the preservation of the homogeneity of a nation or of a government, for "foreigners will bring with them the principles of the government they have imbibed in their youth, or if able to throw them off, it will be in exchange for an unbounded licentiousness, passing, as is usual, from one extreme to another. *It would be a miracle were they to stop precisely at the point of temperate liberty.*" The present generation has fully realized this prophetic declaration of the sagacious Jefferson, and were he living at this time he could not more distinctly and unequivocally express the evils of immigration, and its blighting and withering effect upon republican institutions. He could not have more distinctly shown the evils flowing from the existence of that great German organization in our midst, which has its branches in New York, Philadelphia, Cincinnati, Cleveland, Louisville, Baltimore, Richmond, Pittsburg, and New Orleans, where they have distinctly avowed their object to be to change the Constitution of the United States and to abrogate all laws relative to the observance of the Sabbath.

The framers of the Constitution incorporated into that instrument the principle of *nativism*. They laid down the landmarks by which future generations were to be guided. They declared by that solemn compact, that the President of the United States should be a native born citizen, and, as consequent truths, which necessarily follow from this principle, they established,

1. That the army of the United States should be in his native born American hands.

2. That the navy of the United States should be under native born American control.

3. That treaties should be be organized and made by native born citizens.

4. That Federal appointments and patronage should come from this native born source.

5. That the militia of the several States, when called into the service of the United States, should be under the President's native born command.

6. That only a native born citizen should have the Federal veto power.

They provided farther that the Vice President of the United States should be a native, and thus the Senate, which confirms treaties and the Federal appointments, must be presided over by a native born citizen; and in the event of a tie, a native born only can give the casting vote.

They provided also that Congress and the President should make uniform naturalization laws, that to be a senator, an alien born, must have been naturalized nine years, and to be a member of the House of Representatives he must have been naturalized seven years.

"The President having the appointing power of the Supreme Judges, a native born alone can name the men who are to expound all laws and cases arising under the Constitution, Treaties, and Laws of the United States.

Thus it is seen that the principle of *nativity* was kept constantly in view by the framers of the Constitution, and was thoroughly incorporated in that instrument. Our Revolutionary sires had witnessed the engagement of the German mercenary troops by England, for the British army in America. They had met upon the battle-field the twelve thousand and one hundred Hessians furnished by the landgrave of Hesse-Cassel, the four thousand and eighty-four by the duke of Brunswick, the six hundred and sixty-eight by the prince of Hesse, and the six hundred and seventy by the prince of Waldeck, making in all seventeen thousand five hundred and twenty-six, who had been hired at seven pounds four shillings and four pence sterling per man by the British government to aid in subjugating the American colonies. For seven long years they had struggled to free these colonies from a foreign yoke, and from the tyranny and oppression of a foreign government. They had experienced the arbitrary power of foreign officials, and learned full well the antipathies and animosities of the foreigners to American liberty, and in thus incorporating the principle of nativity, in the magna charta of

American liberty, they have established a principle which experience had taught to be an essential guard against foreign influence and an inestimable requisite to secure the permanency of the American republic.   This principle has re-animated the bosom of the American people, and with the example of our Revolutionary sires before us, who can doubt its ultimate success and permanent re-establishment ?

CHAPTER II.

To borrow the language of that bold and fearless champion of the American reformation (Hon. Wm. R. Smith), "The mass of foreigners who come to this country are incapable of appreciating the policies of our government, they do not sufficiently understand our institutions. Patriotism is natural in a native, but it must be cultivated in a foreigner. Their minds are filled with a vague and indefinite idea of liberty. It is not the liberty of law, but of unrestrained license. Their impressions at home have cultivated and nourished inclinations, and they come here too often to indulge them. The foreigner believes that America is the natural rendezvous for all the exiled patriots, and disaffected and turbulent persons of the earth, and that they are to meet to form plans and concoct schemes to revolutionize all creation and the 'rest of mankind.'" Well, let us see if there is any truth in these suggestions. Here are the solemn resolutions of the German Social Democratic Association of Richmond, Virginia —an association existing in the centre of the "Old Dominion"--the home of the Presidents.

13

Reform in the laws of the general government, as well as in those of the States.

" We demand: 1. Universal suffrage. 2. The election of all officers by the people. 3. The abolition of the Presidency. 4. The abolition of Senates, so that the legislature shall consist of only one branch. 5. The right of the people to recall their representatives (cashier them) at their pleasure. 6. The right of the people to change the Constitution when they like. 7. All lawsuits to be conducted without expense. 8. A department of the government to be set up for the purpose of protecting immigration. 9. A reduced term for acquiring citizenship."

Reform in the foreign relations of the government.

" 1. Abolition of all neutrality. 2. Intervention in favor of every people struggling for liberty."

Reform in what relates to religions.

" 1. A more perfect development of the principle of personal freedom and liberty of conscience; consequently—*a.* Abolition of laws for the observance of the Sabbath; *b.* Abolition of prayers in Congress; *c.* Abolition of oath upon the Bible; *d.* Repeal of laws enacting a religious test before taking an office. 2. Taxation of church property. 3. A prohibition of incorporations of all church property in the name of ecclesiastics."

Reform in the Social Condition.

" 1. Abolition of land monopoly. 2. Ad valorem taxation of property. 3. Amelioration of the condition of the working class— *a.* By lessening the time of work to eight hours for grown persons, and to five hours for children; *b.* by incorporation of mechanics' associations and protective societies; *c.* By granting a preference to mechanics before all other creditors; *d.* By establishing an asylum for superannuated mechanics without means, at the public expense. 4. Education of poor children by the State. 5. Taking possession of the railroads by the State. 6. The promotion of education— *a.* By the introduction of free schools, with the power enforcing the parents to send their children to school, and prohibition of all clerical influence; *b.* By instruction in the German language; *c.* By establishing a German University. 7. The supporting of the slave-emancipation exertions of Cassius M. Clay by Congressional laws. 8. Abolition of the Christian system of punishment, and introduction of the human amelioration system. 9. Abolition of capital punishment."

These are the "fundamental principles of reform of the Social Democratic Society of Germans," and are not confined to Virginia, but are ramified throughout the whole Union, wherever the Germans go.

In proof of which, here are the address and regulation of the American Revolutionary League, adopted at the Revolutionary Congress, held at Philadelphia, from January 29 to February 1, 1852.

"FELLOW CITIZENS: The Congress of the 'American Revolutionary League for Europe' herewith submit the result of their deliberations, to the judgment of the people, all parties of which were represented in that body.

"Earnestly resolved to find the means of terminating the desperate condition of the liberty-thirsting people of Europe, firmly convinced that the first great step to the attainment of this goal, is the cordial co-operation of all who seek it; it was for us to explore the middle ground upon which all parties could honorably and cheerfully unite their forces.

"The conscious determination to achieve a revolution thorough and complete, was the warrant for our actions; and of you, sovereign people, we ask the ratification of this warrant, in the readiness with which you shall erect upon the foundation we have laid, the superstructure of an extensive, yea, a universal fusion of all revolutionary elements.

"Let us, then, be up and doing! Our cause is noble, is sacred. The barriers that cramp the growth of active, intelligent, and high-souled nations are to be stricken down; mankind to be restored to its humanity. Let the motto for the strife be, *Union in the American Revolutionary League.*"

Here are the objects of the League, avowed in a regular form :

" The object of the League shall be the radical liberalization of the European Continent, for which are required :

" 1. The overthrow of monarchy and the establishment of the Republic, because in the Republic alone can all the horrors of tyranny be prevented.

" 2. Direct and universal suffrage, and the recall of representatives by a majority of their constituents ; because this alone secures the supremacy of the popular will in the workings of popular institutions.

" 3. The abolition of standing armies, and inviolability of the right of the people to bear. arms, because the last resource of forcible resistance is the only protection against the last device of forcible usurpation.

" 4. The union for these ends of all persons, associations, parties, and nations, for the annihilation of oppression ; because without such concerted efforts the organized power of the tyrants is invincible."

Art III.—*Means.*

" Sec. 1. Agitation as well in Europe as in America.

" Sec. 2. Accumulation of a revolutionary fund.

" Sec. 3. Formation of armed organizations desirous of entering personally into the struggle and of preparing for it by military exercise."

And these are not the mere idle resolves of a club at a town meeting. It will be seen that they so arranged this league as to extend it to every chief town in the country. So it appears.

" 1. In the principal towns of every State there shall be established a State committee, to consist of the executive board of the revolutionary association there located. If there are several revolutionary associations in such principal town, they shall elect the State committee between them.

" 2. The duty of the State committee shall be to receive the communications of the board, and transmit them to the several associations, and to transmit the proposals of the association to the board, to establish new associations, and generally to make all possible exertions in furtherance of the cause in the State assigned to its care."

And here is the platform of principles and purposes promulgated by the social German democracy of Louisville, Kentucky.

PLATFORM OF THE FREE GERMANS OF LOUISVILLE, KY., ADOPTED
MARCH, 1854.

" 1. *Slavery Question.*—Notwithstanding that we consider slavery to be a political and moral cancer, that will, by and by, undermine all republicanism, we deem its sudden abolition neither possible nor advisable. But we, as republicans and men, demand that the further extension of slavery be not constantly urged, whilst not a single step is taken for its extermination. We demand that at length real proofs be given of the good-will, so often boasted of, to remove the evil; that, in particular, slavery be excluded from all new territories, indiscriminately and forever, which measure Congress is completely entitled to pass according to the Constitution. We demand this the more, as a republican constitution is guaranteed to every new State, and slavery, in truth, cannot be considered a republican element or requisite. We further demand, that all and every one of the laws, indirectly transporting the principle and the influence of slavery in and upon free States, namely, the fugitive slave laws, shall be repealed, as demoralizing and degrading, and as contrary to human rights and to the Constitution. We finally demand that, in all national affairs, the principle of liberty shall be strictly maintained, and even in the several States it be more and more realized by gradual extermination of slavery.

" 2. *Religious Questions.*—We consider the right of free expressions of religious conscience untouchable, as we do the right of free expressions of opinion in general. We therefore accord to the believer the same liberty to make known his convictions, as we do the unbeliever, as long as the rights of others are not violated thereby. But from this very principle of liberty of conscience, we are decidedly opposed to all compulsion, inflicted on dissenting persuasions by laws unconstitutionally restricting the liberty of expression. Religion is a private matter; it has nothing to do with policy; hence it is despotism to compel citizens, by political means, to religious manifestations or omissions contrary to their private persuasions. We, therefore, hold the Sabbath laws, thanksgiving days, prayer in Congress and Legislature, the oath upon the Bible, the introduction of the Bible in the free schools, the exclusion of 'Atheists' from legal acts, &c., as an open violation of human rights as well as of the Constitution, and demand their removal.

" 3. *Measure for the welfare of the people.*—As the foremost of such measures, we consider the free cession of public lands to all settlers; to occupy the natural soil, as exclusive property, this no individual has a right to do; it is, for the time, the common principal fund of that population which inhabits it, and anybody willing to cultivate it has an equal right to appropriate a share of the soil, as far as it is not disposed of, for purposes of common interest. It is high time the ruinous traffic with the public lands should be abolished, that the wasting of them by speculation should cease, and that the indigent people enter upon their rightful possession.

" But if this end shall be fully attained, it will be required to aid poor colonists, at their first settlement, with national means, lest said measures prove useless for these very persons who most need it.

" In the closest connection with the land reform question, stands that of immigration, which, by its general importance, should be raised to the rank of a national affair, and for which a special office of colonization and immigration should be created as a particular department of the United States government. Such a board would have to provide for the various interests of immigrants, who are now helplessly exposed to so many sufferings, and wrongs, and abuses, from the place of embarkation in Europe, to the place of their settlement in America. North America is neglecting herself, when neglecting the immigration, for immigration is the mother of this republic.

" The admission to citizenship must be rendered as easy as possible to the immigrants.

" The welfare to a nation cannot be generally and permanently secured unless its laboring classes be made independent of the oppression of the capitalist. Labor has an incontestible claim to the value of its products. Where it is prevented, by the wants of the necessary capital, to secure this claim, it is, of course, referred to an alliance with capital of others. But if no just agreement can be obtained by this association with the capitalist, then the State, as the arbitrator of all contending interest, has to interfere.

" This must either aid the associations of working men, by credit banks, or mediate between the claims of the laborer and the capitalist, by fixing a minimum of wages equalling the value of the labor, and a maximum of labor answering the demands of humanity. The time of labor shall not exceed ten hours per day.

" In letting our State contracts, the preference should be given, if it can be done without running a risk, to associations of workmen, rather than to single contractors. But when given to single contractors, the latter ought to give security for proper wages to the workmen employed by them.

" In order to enjoy ' life, liberty, and happiness,' all, indiscriminately, must have the use of free schools, for all branches of education, in which, wherever a sufficient number of Germans live, a German teacher should be employed.

" In order that the attainment of justice may no longer remain a privilege for the possession of money, justice must be dispensed without fees.

" 4. *Constitutional Questions.*—Considering, as we do, the American Constitution as the best now in existence, we yet think it neither perfect nor unimproved. In particular, we hold the following amendments and additions likewise acceptable for the State

Constitution, as timely and proper means to check the prevailing corruption, to wit:

"1. All elections, without any exception, should issue directly from the people.

"2. Any eligible citizen of any State may be elected as member of Congress by the citizens of any other State, and likewise may any eligible denizen of any county be elected by the citizens of any other county for a member of the State Legislature.

"3. Any representative and officer may, at any time, be recalled by the majority of his constituents, and replaced by another.

"5. *Free Trade.*—We decidedly profess the principle of free trade, and will support it in all cases where it may be carried through without disadvantage to the people, and when reciprocity is accorded by the other side.

"6. *Foreign Policy.*—The policy of neutrality must cease to be an article of our creed, and ought to be abandoned soon, as contrary to the interests of North America. The rights of American citizens, and immigrants having declared their intention to become citizens, must the more energetically be protected in foreign countries, since every American appears to monarchical and despotical governments as a representative of revolution against despotism, and this republic ought to honor this point of view as the only one worthy and legitimate.

"7. *Rights of Women.*—The Declaration of Independence says that 'All men are born equal, and endowed with inalienable rights, and to these, belong life, liberty, and the pursuit of happiness.' We repeatedly adopt this principle, and are of the opinion that women, too, are among 'all men.'

"8. *Rights of Free Persons.*—In the free States, the color of the skin cannot justify a difference of legal rights. There are not born two men of equal color, but still less, two men of unequal rights.

"9. *Penal Laws.*—It is our opinion, that all penal laws can only have the purpose of correction, but never the absurd purpose of expiation. We, therefore, consider the penalty of death, which excludes the possibility of correction, to be as irrational as barbarous."

All these demands are antagonistic to the fundamental principles and established usages of the government. The Bible is repudiated, the sanctity of an oath is rejected, the observance of the Sabbath is enumerated among the evils which these Germans seek to correct. The presidency is to be abolished, all powers are to be vested exclusively in the masses, and the Constitution must give way to the whims and caprices of the people. All the safeguards which protect the minority in the enjoyment of their rights and privileges are to be broken down, and every right, privilege and immunity, all laws, the policy of the government, the institutions of the country, and its relations with other countries, are to be dependent upon the will of an uncontrollable and licentious majority; the government is to become " a heterogeneous, incoherent mass."

These organizations have not stopped with a mere enumeration of their principles. They have boldly entered the political arena, asserted their right to share with us in legislation and with a zeal and determination worthy of a better cause, sought to engraft upon our institutions the " principles which they imbibed in early youth." The abjuration of their allegiance to the country of their birth has not divested them of their principles. The oath of allegiance to ours, has not infused into them the spirit of our government. They have left home and kindred, severed associations, and cut asunder the ties of relationship, but the principles they "imbibed in youth," still cling to them. They have brought with them the " maxims of absolute monarchies," or exchanged them "for an unbounded licentiousness." Nor are the Germans the only class of foreigners who have organized for the purpose of concentrating their political power, and directing that power at the government. As early as 1814 the Irish were troublesome to our people, and were not unfrequently denounced as such by the press of those days. A friend has handed the author a copy of the "Herald of Liberty," published at Augusta, Maine, bearing date April 30th, 1814, speaking of the envoys sent to Gottenburg, to negotiate peace with Great Britain; it says in a letter from Washington of April 12th,

"Whenever any measure displeases these licensed calumniators, they are as insolent and vituperous against government as they are mean and fawning when they are pleased. It is known to Mr. Madison, who has American feeling, that at a late meeting of the Tammany Savage society in New York, a motion was made to denounce him, *á la mode de Robespierre*, for his message to Congress for the repeal of the embargo law, and that it was negatived only by a small majority. This society is principally made up of the fæces of the sewers of Ireland, &c. I am confident the President would consent to the introduction of any article in a treaty of peace which should interdict every species of naturalization, for he knows it to be a fact, 'that these aliens have been the great cause of our troubles, and disgrace, and until the country is rid of them it will foster serpents in its bosom.'"

Forty years ago the Tammany Savage Society, composed of Irishmen, denounced President Madison, for having recommended to Congress the repeal of the embargo laws. At that period there were not two hundred thousand immigrants in the country, yet they were organized into societies and into communities, and were, says the writer, "the great cause of our troubles and disgrace." The immigrants of 1814 were far superior to those of the present day. They came to seek an asylum in this land of constitutional liberty, and not to govern it; they came to enjoy the blessings of our laws and not to make laws; but even then so thoroughly had they imbibed the sympathies and feelings and principles of their respective races, that it was impossible to divest themselves of them. Since then the races have degenerated, and the immigrants of the present day are but the inferior specimens of these degenerated races. The Dublin "Evening Mail" of April 13th, 1855, contains an account of a recent election in Cavan county, Ireland, which furnishes us with a striking illustration of the character of the Irish elector at home, it says:

"A body of upwards of two thousand men marched into the town, brandishing formidable sticks, in a truly independent manner, and shouting for the tenant right and Hughes. Three Roman Catholic clergymen accompanied them, on horseback, and also, it was stated, ninety voters for Mr. Hughes. Other large bodies followed in quick succession, and the approach to the court-house was soon almost blocked up—the aspect of affairs which had previously worn a rather quiet appearance, becoming very visibly altered. A lane was formed of fellows brandishing their sticks, through which the voters going to the court-house were obliged to pass. The position of soldiers and the police, was somewhat altered, in order to keep this mob back. After a while they began to seize voters and drag them into Mr. Hughes's committee rooms.

*　　*　　*　　*　　*　　*　　*　　*

"A party of armed men went, between nine and ten o'clock on Tuesday night, to the house of an elector at Ballinagh, for the purpose of making him promise to vote for Mr. Hughes. He refused to do so, and then they demanded that he should swear not to vote for Mr. Burrowes, and on his refusing this also, THEY THREW HIM ACROSS THE FIRE, AND HELD HIM THERE UNTIL THE FLESH WAS BURNED OFF HIS RIBS.

"The Catholic party endeavored to force a man named John Corr to vote against his conscience. After being imprisoned and maltreated for two hours, the account says : 'They put him on his knees, and tried to compel him to swear that he would not vote for Mr. Burrowes, but he resolutely refused to do so. They then dragged him back into town to the court-house, in the roughest manner and kicking him and knocking out one of his teeth. They detained a tally-ticket for him in the liberal committee room ; he refused to take it into his hand, and it was thrust into his breast. He was then brought into the booth, but he objected to vote, on the ground that he had been kept under constraint ; after sitting some time in the court-house, he was enabled, with the aid of a gentleman named Gaffney, to return to his home.' "

It must be borne in mind, that these outlaws are the electors of Ireland, and claimed as the respectable and intelligent portion of the population. If they prostitute the ballot-box at home, what may we expect from the less intelligent and more reckless, who flock to our shores by thousands?

In late years, immigration has greatly increased. Foreign organizations have become more numerous and formidable, and their attempts to obtain political power more frequent.

At a charter election, held in the city of New York, a few years ago, the following hand-bill was published by the Irish organization, and extensively circulated, to wit:

"Irishmen to your post, or you will lose America. By perseverance you may become its rulers. By negligence you will become its slaves. Your own country was lost by submitting to ambitious rulers. This beautiful country you gain by being firm and united. Vote the tickets Alexander Stewart, Alderman ; Edward Flannigan, Assessor, both true Irishmen."

About the same time, at an election in the county of Lasalle, Illinois, a body of Irish immigrants, numbering about two thousand, brought forward and supported an Irishman for the office of sheriff, in opposition to an American of the same national politics, and of much longer residence in the country, and elected him, by upwards of one thousand majority.

In the town of Patterson, New Jersey, but a few years ago, an election was held, in which the foreigners elected thirty-three out of thirty-seven township officers.

Numerous instances could be cited where the leaders of political parties have been compelled to submit to the decision of the foreign population of their respective election districts, which of the candidates should be run by their party for an office ; and the political history of our country, for a few years back, is full of instances, in which the foreign organizations have demanded of the candidates pledges. One of the most remarkable is that which occurred in the city of Baltimore, just previous to the election for members of Congress, in 1853. The German organization of this city addressed a series of questions to each of the candidates, and demanded of them written responses to the interrogatories. They were organized and determined to cast their votes *as a body of Germans,* for him who answered most satisfactorily. The following is the correspondence between the organization and the Honorable Henry May, for whom they cast their votes, and the reader will perceive that the purpose, on the part of the Germans, was to preserve their organization as Germans, to retain their distinctive characteristics, and to force, by the power of

2

their organization, an American candidate for office to yield to them:

LETTER TO MR. MAY.

BALTIMORE, *June 23d*, 1853.

DEAR SIR: At the third meeting of the German Citizens' Convention, being organized to *advise the German voting Community* of Baltimore HOW TO CAST THEIR VOTES at the next election, it was unanimously resolved to authorize the Executive Committee to inquire of every gentleman having submitted the use of his name as a candidate for Congress, subject to a Democratic nomination:

1st. If he is convinced of the *justice and necessity of our organization ?*

2d. If he openly pledges himself to represent us in Congress, according to the laws of equality and justice, without any preference to native born American citizens.   A written reply is requested.

By order of the President.

S. B. WENTZ, *Secretary.*

MR. MAY'S REPLY TO THE GERMANS.

BALTIMORE, *June 23d*, 1853.

SIR: I have this morning received your letter of this date, proposing to me two questions.   I am prompt to reply.

To the first, that I have not been favored with a perusal of the constitution of your Convention, but as far as I understand its principles, I am convinced both of the *justness and expediency of your organization!*

To the second: That I pledge myself, if elected to a seat in the Congress of the United States, to represent my constituents according to the laws of equality and justice, under the Federal Constitution, without giving any preference to native-born American citizens.

As an American citizen or representative, I shall ever stand firmly, I trust, upon the broad basis of equal rights, justice and protec-

tion to my fellow-citizens who enjoy that title under the Constitu-
of our Union.

I am very respectfully,
Your obedient servant,   HENRY MAY.

To J. B. WENTZ, ESQ.,
Sec. of German Convention, Balt., Md.

A pledge of belief in the "justice and necessity" of the German organization was demanded of each candidate, and the avowed object of the organization, as stated in the letter of the secretary, was "to advise the German voting community, of Baltimore, how to cast their votes."

Mr. May says, in a card published subsequent to the publication of this correspondence, that he "was glad to find that all the candidates, except one, agreed in the same views I (he) expressed." Mr. Preston, who was the candidate in opposition to the Honorable Joshua Vansant, denounced, in his reply to the interrogatories, the object and purposes of the convention. Mr. Vansant concurred in opinion with Mr. May, and both were elected, and both, by way of attesting their sincere belief in the "justice and necessity" of German organizations, were opposed to the bill to prohibit the shipment of foreign paupers.

The Philadelphia Pennsylvanian, of April 7th, 1856 (a Democratic paper), in speaking of the frequent attempts of foreigners to control the election of delegates to political conventions, says:

"The two prominent causes which led to the organization of the Native party, and gave it great strength, were the placing of candidates in nomination, who possessed no one pre-requisite for office, and the indignation occasioned by the moving of large gangs of unnaturalized persons from poll to poll, to rob, by their votes, competent citizens of their rights. This latter evil, we regret to say, still exists. We have been informed, that it is the intention of a few depraved and worthless members of the Democratic party, to practise this great outrage at some of the polls to-night. If such a great wrong be attempted, it should be resisted at every hazard. The Democratic party cannot be kept intact, if the legal voters attached to it are to have their votes rendered nugatory, by the introduction of fraudulent tickets into the ballot-boxes, voted by aliens. We should have honesty at our primary elections, and wherever an alien attempts to vote, he should be prosecuted on the charge of inciting to a breach of the peace. We hope that all good Democrats will resent the degradation that must attach to our party, if unnaturalized voters attempt to control our delegate elections."

Such authority as this cannot be doubted nor gainsayed. It comes from one who has been unremittingly a friend of the alien, and who is strenuously opposed to any further legislation upon the subject of naturalization.

The Galveston Zeitung of August 19th, 1855, the organ of the Germans of Texas, contains the following manifesto to the Germans of that State.

"You have often observed that the continual clashing between natives and foreigners might easily come to a general eruption, which would result disastrously to the Germans, unless we consider in time the proverb that "He who desires peace should prepare for war.

"The Cincinnati April scenes, and those at Columbus, have shown that the police in such cases are not fully sufficient for our guard, or suppression of the mob. In such cases, we must depend upon ourselves to defend our families and property, as is our duty and right. Without an organization this is impossible. In the moment of an attack it is too late to form such an organization; our duty is to organize beforehand. I therefore submit the following propositions:

"1st. To form in every town where there is sufficient German population, one or more guard companies who shall furnish their arms.

" 2d. The uniform must be everywhere the same, to preserve equality. The uniform is necessary to prevent confusion and to distinguish our friends.

" 3d. The arms must be everywhere the same, and we recommend as the best the arms of the Turners and revolvers.

" 4th. A member of any company shall be recognized as a member wherever there be such a company formed. All the companies in the United States must be in connection with one chief or leader.

" 5th. The decade system is the most commendable, i. e., every ten members to constitute one decade, and make one leader, who in case of necessity can call together his nine comrades. The leaders, then elect their officers. Five decades would be enough for one company."

This is in direct contravention to the laws of the country, under whose protection they live. It is neither their duty nor their right, to organize as Germans. They claim to be citizens of the United States, and as such are entitled to its protection. Their organization as a society or a community of Germans is inconsistent with the institutions of the country, and any effort to protect themselves, not from any armed body of natives, for none has dared to interrupt them in the enjoyment of either, their social or political rights, but to protect themselves from the *influence* of the free, liberal, enlightened and republican institutions, by cutting off and preventing intercourse between themselves and the natives, is utterly subversive of these institutions.

Their association and free intermingling with the

natives is disastrous to many of the habits, customs, and peculiarities, which they have brought with them from their fatherland, and which they desire to transmit to their children, and hence it is that these exclusive organizations are adhered to.

During the fall of 1855, at an election held at one of the interior towns of Texas, the Germans marched in a body to the polls. The Hon. Mr. Wilcox, formerly a member of the House of Representatives from Mississippi, gives the following account of the occurrence.

" On the day of election here, the Germans paraded their flag (instead of the national) through the streets. They marched in procession through the city, chanting German national airs. The French singing the Marseilles hymn. I never felt so mortified and chagrined in the whole course of my life. Yet, it is said, we have nothing to fear from German influence."

The German political club of Cleveland, Ohio, in 1852, adopted the following resolution by way of approving of the offer of " material aid " by the free negroes of that city.

" Whereas, The colored people in their meeting held on the 17th inst., have expressed their sympathy with the German nation by a resolution to actually aid the German national coalition, the German political club resolve ;

" 1. To express its hearty thanks, and avail itself of this opportunity to declare the conviction that the German people, as soon as they shall have obtained the Democratic republic in the coming struggle, use all means which are adapted to abolish slavery, an institution which is so wholly repugnant to the principles of true democracy.

" 2. This resolution shall be published in all the newspapers of the city."

On Sunday the 23d September, 1855, the German democrats of the city of New York, thus carrying out the principle in their German constitution of abrogating the Sabbath, assembled in general convention, composed of delegates from the several wards in the city, to take into consideration the welfare of the German organization, and to nominate candidates for the city and State offices, or to exact pledges from some of the candidates.

The convention was organized by the election of the following officers :

President, WILLIAM LETZEISER, of 12th ward.
1st Vice President, GUSTAVE SCHOENKE, of 17th ward.
2nd " " A. I. NEI, of 22nd ward.
1st Secretary, DR. CHARLES A. KLEIN, of 17th ward.
2nd " DR. HAENLEIM, of 20th ward.

The convention then resolved to take speedy steps for the organization of committees in the various wards, so that the German vote might be thoroughly canvassed, and polled to its full strength. Various speeches were made, exhorting the Germans to unity, and encouraging them to assert their principles, and " dare maintain them." And on Sunday, 30th September, another German convention in the same city asssembled for a similar purpose.

The German citizens of Galena, Illinois, held a meeting at the Court-house in that city, during the month of January last, which was addressed by Mr. Stibolt, the editor of the " Vorwarts," a German liberal paper; and after his address, the following, among other resolutions, were subscribed to by one hundred and fifty-seven persons of German birth.

" *Resolved*, That we, as true democrats, for the present will preserve our independence of all political parties, and go only for principle.

" *Resolved*, That slavery is a curse to our beloved republic, a stain for a free nation ; and that we, therefore, will stand with all free men, shoulder to shoulder, fighting against the propagation of slavery over free territory, and against the Nebraska bill and its consequences.

" *Resolved*, That the slavery question.is the most urgent and important question of the present time.

" *Resolved*, That we will support only such candidates for State officers as are opposed to the Nebraska bill, and to Know-Nothingism."

Did true democracy admit of a German construction in this country, the Revolution would long since have proved a curse, instead of a blessing. When foreigners, enjoying our hospitality—as they do, assume to set up a standard of " Democracy " which proscribes a portion of their benefactors, it is high time that the birth-right qualification for office and voting, should be established.

In 1853, according to the New Orleans Creole, a Mr. Wippretcht (a real jaw-breaking German name), made a speech to his " constitutional" fellow " citizens," at or near New Braunfels, Texas, in which he belabored the native-born Americans for their arrogance in claiming to have any voice whatever in the government of Western Texas, as that country, according to Mr. *Whiptretch*, had been first settled by the Germans, and therefore belonged exclusively to them. In concluding his speech, Mynheer W. said, " Now, let us manfully and firmly oppose the arrogant assumptions and overbearings of these natives. Let us oppose their further extension of this slave-holding population in Western Texas, for we have cultivated and settled this country before the natives thought of doing so."

These disorganizing sentiments have spread with fearful success. Read the following extract from a speech of Mr. Rœdel to a German meeting in the city of New York, during the month of January, 1855.

"BRETHREN: For the first time I speak in an assembly like this. We have not all the same language, but our feelings are the same; they unite us here with the American people. For the advancement of these sentiments we must not only unite with them in speeches, but also in acts. In our country we have fought for liberty and many of us have lost, in battle, our fathers, brothers, or sons. Here we are free, but not free enough; we want the liberty of living. [Applause.] We have fought in Germany for liberty of speech and the liberty of the press. The German press is against us in this movement; but we need not care for what those papers say; we must act on our own hook. Here we have social liberty, liberty of speech, and liberty of the press; and when we want anything that is just, we are bound to obtain it. [Applause.] If you don't know your rights yet, hunger will teach them to you. You don't get bread nor wood, and there is plenty of them. At our revolution in June, we obtained three months' credit, because we were two hundred thousand strong. *I have nothing further to say than to advise you to put in practice the principles of the social Republic.* The 'Tribune' said to-day, that the rich would give a million, if they were forced to it; but now they will hold their money in their pockets, and refuse to give it up. When the wolf is hungry he has no consideration, and takes his food fearlessly where he finds it; it must be the same with the masses. Help yourselves, and then God will help you. We must act as the wolf, and we do not want any auxiliaries! Let us act by ourselves."

He had nothing further to say than to advise the Germans " to put in practice the principles of the social Republic." And as a means to hasten this result, he said, " let us act by ourselves."

Hunger was the excuse for the promulgation of such sentiments. Hunger warranted, in the opinion of this imported socialist, the enforcement of the "principles of the social republic," that is, the abrogation of the Sabbath, and the abolition of oaths. Hunger justified the removal of all moral restraints, and a total disregard of all laws. If the permanency of the American Republic is to depend upon the appetites of its alien population, the contingency will soon arise when it will become necessary for them to "put in practice the principles of the social republic." " Here," said the orator, " we are free, but not free enough." " We are," he should have added, "under the restraint of law, and have sworn to support the Constitution ; these are but relics of ancient feudalism, alike unjust and tyrannical. We need no Constitution, no laws, no Sabbath, no Bible, no courts of law, no President, nor a legislature. All laws are curses, and all rulers are tyrants." Such are the sentiments of the social German democracy. Such are the principles which the German population seek to establish.

During the past year, Irish conventions have assembled in Boston, New York, and Philadelphia. These conventions held their sessions in secret, and are composed of delegates representing subordinate bodies or societies, which exist within certain prescribed limits. The Boston convention was probably composed of delegates representing the societies in several of the New England States; the New York, comprised New York, and the Philadelphia, Pennsylvania. No authentic history of these conventions, how organized, and for what purposes, have, as yet, been published ; sufficient, however, is known to conjecture, with some degree of accuracy, the rules and regulations which govern the representative and subordinate bodies.

The following is a sketch of the proceedings of the New York convention, as reported by the "New York Daily Times." It was in session for several days, and the only knowledge of the proceedings was obtained through the ingenuity of the newspaper conductors.

"The various committees appointed the previous day, submitted their respective reports, which were all, after some debate, adopted. The committee on the platform, and the one appointed to draft an address, made reports, which gave rise to long and animated debates. Both reports were finally adopted with some amendments.

"A large amount of general and necessary work was transacted, but the principal and most important question before the body, was that in reference to the appointment of a supreme directory. The consideration of this matter occupied much time, but was not, we believe, concluded. Upon the necessity of such a measure, the delegates seem to be all agreed. The contest, if any should arise, will be about the *men.*

"The convention finally determined not to admit, as delegates, the representatives of the Emmett Monument Association; not that they doubted their loyalty in the least, but because they believe they have no 'power to admit others than those duly appointed by the State organization of the Emigrant Society.

"The platform and address which have been adopted differ but little from those promulgated at Boston, some six months ago. The former explains the plan of operations, and ignores all action on the part of the society not in strict conformity with the laws of the United States. The address calls upon all Irishmen to rally once more for the redemption of their fatherland, now that the time for triumph has arrived—beseeches them to drop all disputes, forget all differences, and unite, Catholics and Protestants, for the attainment of the end desirable—an Irish republic."

Among the important questions which this convention had under consideration, was that in "reference to the appointment of a supreme directory." Upon the necessity, says the report, of such a measure, the delegates seem to be all agreed. How this "directory" was to be appointed, and for what purposes, is not known. It is to be presumed, that it is to have the general supervision of the affairs of the Irish organization in the State of New York. The State of New York has a governor, legislature, and all necessary officers to protect its citizens in the enjoyment of their rights, and with the State authorities the native citizens are content to entrust their lives, liberty, and property. But the Irishmen, many of whom are not, as yet, entitled to the rights of citizenship, deem it necessary for their protection, or for the purpose of enforcing their schemes or principles, that a "supreme directory," composed solely of Irishmen, should be established. It may be that this "supreme directory" is a central body having jurisdiction over the Irish organizations throughout the country, and that the New York convention was acting, so far as regards this matter, in conjunction with the other conventions, which had assented. If this be so, it is antagonistic to the spirit of the national government—for the government recognizes no authority higher than itself, over any portion of its citizens. If these conventions had in view any charitable purpose they might be excusable, but any organization of foreigners, whether secret or open, is to be regarded with suspicion in a republic.

A correspondent of the "Philadelphia Ledger," a paper neutral in politics, writing from New York during the session of the convention, says:

" A plan, I am told, has been submitted ' to reach the heart of the British Lion,' through his Canadian lungs. Five thousand able-bodied Hibernians are represented to be all ready for enrollment to march to Canada, in order to co-operate with some Russian demonstration, said to be organizing on the northwest coast. Money sufficient to defray expenses, it is further said, has already been raised, and the only thing remaining to be done is to find a man in whom all can have confidence as a leader. Secrecy being one of the greatest things needed now, pains are taken to keep out of the newspapers anything like a real record of what is in the wind. But the facts here related may be relied upon. It is probable, however, that the whole scheme will 'burst up,' owing to the personal jealousies and personal hatreds which govern the convention.

" Another rumor may as well be mentioned ; it is a wild one, but there may be 'something in it.' An agent of Russia is said to be the financial agent, and the chief engineer of the whole concern. Who he is, or where he is, I can't say, but it is thought to be something of an object to get up an invasion of Canada, in order to distract the allies at home, and possibly compel England to transport a portion of her army in the Crimea to the North American colonies."

If these conjectures be correct, and there has been no denial, it would seem that the great object of the convention was to organize secretly an army of Irishmen, either for the purpose of commencing hostilities against some friendly government, or against this. But the chief dangers to be apprehended arise from the fact of the existence of any such organizations, whether they be civil or military. No candid man will gainsay the declaration, that if foreigners reside among us as foreigners, without assimilating, in any manner, with the American character, that sound policy and true statesmanship demand the immediate enactment of

laws, either prohibiting their immigration, or restricting
their political privileges. If it be the purpose of this
convention to organize an army, do they organize it as
Americans or as foreigners? American citizens have
no such right, and certainly foreigners should not
have. Even upon the hypothesis that no violation of
the laws of the land was contemplated, and that no
improper motive incited these foreigners to organize,
and that no treasonable purpose was in view, does it
comport with the policy of the government to permit
such organizations to exist. The riots of '44, and those
of Cincinnati and Louisville, should warn us of their
danger to life and property.

The ostensible object of these conventions was to
devise the ways and means to liberate Ireland. In
relation to which the "Philadelphia Pennsylvanian" (in
politics, democratic) comments thus:

"We strongly suspect that the organizations, now under process,
have an object *much nearer home* than the 'Gem of the Sea.'
'Coming events cast their shadows before,' and the boastful follies
of an indiscreet mind, often serve as an index to the object to be
attained by commotion. * * * Already has our government,
with the most commendable integrity, broken up combinations
against the peace of sister republics, and thus declared the illegality
of such associations. If our own native citizens cannot so infringe
the law, why do those of a particular nativity claim the privilege?
They are our equals before the law, and not our superiors, nor do
they possess a single privilege not common to ourselves. If their
design is not against the peace of England, we must look for the
power of the organization to be exercised politically against ourselves. It can have but one or the other of these objects, and as
both are alike criminal, we shall resist both to the last. We do not
hesitate to say, that we are distrustful of its purpose, and base our

suspicions upon the knowledge we have of actors in previous organizations."

The opinion of the "Pennsylvanian" is based upon a "knowledge of the actors in previous organizations." It is certainly true, that if their design is not against the peace of England, it will, sooner or later, be exercised politically against this government.

It matters not what purposes prompt the foreigners to organize into separate and exclusive societies or communities. Such associations must ultimately endanger the perpetuity of American institutions. No such organization can, none ever has, existed long without engendering animosities amongst the members thereof, or between themselves and the natives. It is contrary to the laws of nature for any two people so unlike physically, mentally, morally, socially, and politically, to live together under the same jurisdiction, and, at the same time, live as a separate and distinct people. A conflict must come. The history of the world is replete with such collisions. It is a conflict of races, and the struggle is for superiority. The Hungarian war of 1849 and '50, arose from a conflict between the Sclavonians and Magyars; neither were willing to yield up their respective nationalities; each appealed to Austria for aid, and both were subjugated by Austria. The early history of England furnishes several instances of a conflict of races, and no country has escaped them, where the population was made up of different races, and those races preserved their respective characteristics; even our own country affords a most striking illustration of the incompatibility of races. The Indians have almost entirely disappeared, but they yielding nothing. It was a bloody conflict, and not yet terminated.

The identity of the population of any country is essential to the preservation of good order, to the perpetuity of its established institutions, and to the protection of its citizens. A mere difference of opinion as to the temporary policy of a government, such as frequently occurs between two political parties, does not destroy the identity of the people, though frequently such conflicts of opinion merely are not unattended with trouble, even threatening the safety of the government.

To return to the consideration of the Irish organizations. In the foregoing, the objects of these organizations have been merely conjectured; but notwithstanding the guard of secrecy which covered up and hid all their operations and purposes, they have not escaped detection. The judicial investigation which recently took place at Cincinnati, into the alleged Irish fillibustering movement, has given to the public sufficient of their internal regulations, and revealed their purposes to an extent which should excite alarm in the bosom of every true American. The Cincinnati organization is denominated the Robert Emmett Club, and it is more than probable that this is the designation in all other portions of the country.

Here is the address of this club:

ADDRESS OF THE ROBERT EMMETT BRANCH OF THE IRISH EMIGRANT AID SOCIETY OF OHIO, TO THE IRISHMEN OF THE BUCKEYE STATE.

"FELLOW EXILES : The sun of Ireland's independence, so long obscured by the clouds of adversity, is bursting through the darkness

of centuries, and may soon shine in splendor over a liberated nation!
For ages our fathers fought and bled in vain—for centuries they suffered the penalties of subjection to the stranger, and died in the confident hope that the men of succeeding ages would avenge their
wrongs and liberate the nation from the oppression of the Anglo-
Norman robber.

"The day for which they sighed and prayed has come, and the
spirits of our martyred dead call on us from above, to blot out the
shame of centuries, and lift our dear old nation up to happiness and
freedom.   The voice of the exiled Celt has gone forth from the bay of
Boston, to cheer the drooping, to stimulate the slothful, and unite
all Irishmen in one grand rally for the freedom of Ireland !   Shall
we, then, the Irish inhabitants of the West, hold back in such an
hour, and in such a cause ?   Shall the opportune moment be lost,
and the day that God gives us for vengeance be spent in doubt and
fear ?

"No ! by the faith our race, by the bones of our insulted dead !
by the memory of Clintarf! by the massacre of Mullaghmart and
Tara! by the recollection of the starved millions of '46 and '47! by
the glorious deeds of Wexford and Vinegar Hill! by the ruthless
perfidy of the Saxon! by the untimely death of Tone and Fitzgerald!
and the uninscribed tomb of Emmett, vengeance is ours, and we
shall repay !

"Awake, then Irishmen of Ohio ! and to the rescue.   The day of
England's tribulation is now—the withering breath of an angry God
is upon her, scourging her for the robberies, the murders, the massacres of ages, and dissolving her power like snow before the warm
sun !   With the opportunity presented, and freedom before us, shall
we, the exiled sons of a crushed and lacerated mother, remain forever helots of every people who wish to put the yoke upon our necks,
toil through reproach and opprobrium, in the rags of servitude, and
die with slavery's fetters on our limbs, without an effort to efface
the black and bitter memory of the past ?   Ireland speaks to us
through the Massachusetts convention.   Shall we not heed her call,
and organize as she directs ?   Cincinnati has already adopted the
Massachusetts platform and plan of action, and is duly authorized
to organize the State of Ohio.   The Robert Emmett Club of Cincin-

nati, therefore, calls on you, Irishmen, to organize clubs in every city, town, and village in the State, on the above plan, and every necessary information will be furnished you here, on application to our secretary. When the State is thus organized into clubs, a State convention will be called, and a State directory elected who shall manage the funds and other business of the society.

" Irishmen, let no man fail or falter now. The work is light if action be united, and every man do his duty.

" Oh ! how long have we wept over the tale of sorrow, that weekly came to us from our own Innisfail, and how ardently we watched for any movement that would cast a ray of hope across the polluted waters of Irish politics ; but never in our most ardent imaginings and loftiest dreaming, did we hope for such a grand opportunity, as the God of nations gives this day to the land our of love. Let us, then, if we are men, prepare to accept the boon, and grasp the liberty of Ireland with a strong and armed hand. The man who now holds back, was made for a slave, and deserves the coward's fate.

" The men of Massachusetts have set a noble example, one worthy of imitation by every State in the Union, and be assured that nothing will give the true friends of the cause such buoyant hopes as to find that Ohio is firm in the ranks of Irish patriotism.

" Let each man's motto be, to cultivate the friendship of his neighbor, to be sober, prudent, and hopeful, and we cannot fail.

" ' They win the .fight that must be won,
The freedom of our land, which they so well begun.'

" Signed in behalf of the Club.

" DANIEL CONAHAN, President.

" EDWARD KENIFECK, Secretary.

" CINCINNATI, Sept. 27, 1855."

This address discloses the whole plan of operation. It was circulated secretly among the Irish population of Ohio, and only gained publicity through a judicial investigation. It exhibits the bitter hostility which the Irish retain for the Anglo-Norman race, which it styles " robbers," and attempts to arouse their ancient animosities by appealing to their prejudices, and by recounting the past injuries which the Irish people as a nation have received from the hands of England.

That they should retain a vivid recollection of the massacres of Mullaghmart and Tara, of the glorious deeds of Wexford and Vinegar Hill, and of the death of Tone and Fitzgerald, is natural enough, but that they should as American citizens, seek to make England atone for the past, affords indisputable evidence of their want of fidelity to the government under whose protection they live. They have abjured absolutely all allegiance to any and every government, and sworn to support the Constitution and the laws of the United States.

The following is the oath of the Robert Emmett Club, which was made public during the Cincinnati investigation:

THE OATH.

"In the awful presence of God, I do voluntarily declare and promise, that I shall use my endeavors to form a brotherhood amongst Irishmen of all persuasions, for to uproot and overthrow English government in Ireland; and I furthermore declare that neither hopes, fears, rewards nor punishments, shall ever induce me to make known any of the secrets of this Order. To all this I most solemnly pledge my most sacred honor."

Are not these developments sufficient to create alarm and apprehension? Who can calculate the strength of these organizations? The Irish population of this country now numbers a million, of that number nearly six hundred thousand are males, and who knows but there are six hundred thousand armed Irishmen in our midst, bound together by a solemn oath and sworn to keep their secrets inviolable? Should not the government interfere and break up these organizations? They have committed a thousand times greater infractions of the neutrality laws, than anything charged upon Mr. Crampton or the British consuls at Philadelphia, New York, and Cincinnati.

"If ever it was incumbent upon a government to preserve its honor, and strangle the serpent of sedition hissing under its very eye, now is the time for the Federal Executive to act. Every leader of these Irish and German leagues, from Robert Tyler down to the most insignificant Pat or Hans, should be arrested, indicted, tried and punished. Mr. Tyler has not the excuse of ignorance which may be pleaded by his dupes, who will be surprised at the heinousness of their offence, when the veil falls from their features of their false prophet. Are we to prevent enlistments under the garb of Emigrant Aid Societies, which have for their avowed objects the invasion of Ireland or interference in the affairs of other European governments?"

And as a measure of safety for the future, should not the legislative department of the government interfere? A few years more and the golden opportunity may have passed away.

John Mitchel, formerly the editor of "The Citizen," said to the Irishmen of this country,

"Be careful not to truckle in the smallest particular to American prejudices. Yield not a single jot of your own; for you have as good a right to your prejudices as they."

The St. George Society, a society of Englishmen in the State of New York, at its anniversary meeting in 1852 adopted the following address to her majesty the Queen of England.

" *May it please your Majesty.*

"We, your Majesty's most dutiful and loyal subjects, a committee recently appointed by the St. George Society of the State of New York, a corporate body, formed for the relief and support of our countrymen who may be in distress within this State, humbly beg leave to tender to your majesty, in the name of our society, our most grateful acknowledgments for the high mark of favor which your majesty has been so graciously pleased to confer upon us, in permitting a copy of the portrait of your majesty, by Winterhalter, to be made for our society. This signal proof of the benevolent regard which your majesty has condescended to entertain for a body of your majesty's subjects, who, though removed from the immediate sphere of your majesty's beneficent rule, and the lustre of your majesty's bright example, yield to none in devotion to your majesty, and your majesty's illustrious family, will be regarded with sentiments which so gracious an act must call forth. In venturing, therefore, to intrude upon your majesty with this expression of their gratitude, the committee beg to assure your majesty that the members of this society, though far from the land of their fathers and of their love, can never cease to think of it with tenderness, and that the prayers which they offer to God from their home in this friendly republic, for the long continuance of your majesty's health and prosperity, flow from hearts as loyal, and are uttered by lips as true, as can be found in almost any part of your majesty's almost boundless dominions."

Many of the members of this society are naturalized citizens, and have resided in this country long enough to have become attached to the government, yet in the address above quoted, they declare, "*They yield to none in devotion to your* (her) *majesty,*" and that " *though far from the land of their fathers and of their love,* can never cease to think of it (the British government) with tenderness." They further declare that these sentiments "*flow* from hearts as loyal, and are uttered by lips as true," as any of her majesty's subjects. The ancient maxim is truly verified, "*once an Englishman always an Englishman.*"

CHAPTER III.

I⊤ is proper, before proceeding any further, to review the "Kossuth Mania," which but a few years ago convulsed the country throughout its length and breadth.

Kossuth was an exile from his fatherland. He came to this country by invitation, and by his eloquent appeals excited the sympathies of the whole people, and by his representations enlisted many in his cause. His fame had been wafted across the " briny deep," and our people, always sympathizing with the oppressed, received him with open arms, and extended to him the hand always ready to strike in defence of liberty. But for what purpose did he come? Did he come to live amongst us and to become identified with a republican government? No. Did he come to this land of constitutional liberty to share with us in the enjoyment of its privileges and blessings? No. He came with the arrogance of a conqueror, though an exile. He came not as a pupil, but as a teacher, and what he came to teach us, we can best learn from his own declarations. In a speech delivered in England, but a few days previous to his departure for this country, he said :

47

" I suppose it is known now that the policy of England and of
the United States can unite ; and when they are united, I myself
hope that without wars, the interest of mankind, by that means,
will be secured.   *   *   *   *   *   *

" When I go to the United States, I will consider it to be one of
my duties to try if there cannot be an humble opportunity for this
Union, as I was an humble opportunity for the promulgation of the
solidarity sentiment of nations for the principles of liberty."

In that same speech he characterizes Washington's
policy of non-intervention, as " the letter-marque of despotism." He said :

"That is the principle—the sovereign right of every nation to
dispose of itself.   But this is not the non-intervention which would
be defined by these words : I do not care whatever be the fate of
humanity—whatever the disposal of the world may do with Europe,
or with its liberty, because my principle is non-intervention. That,
I say, is not non-intervention ; it is the *letter-marque of despotism ;*
it would be an assurance to society to carry with certainty the vic-
tory to despotism."

The reader must bear in mind the fact, that though
he asserted he believed in the principle of non-intervention or neutrality, so far as regards the affairs of other
nations, yet he denounced the principle of non-intervention as enunciated by Washington, as the " *letter-marque
of despotism.*"

When he arrived at New York, a Doctor Somebody
addressed him as follows :

"For my part, and I ask no one to be responsible for what I say,
although I honestly believe that I speak the sentiments of the great
mass of my fellow-countrymen, and especially the sentiments of
those *three millions of stalwart, able-bodied, young men of America
whom our laws have designed for military purposes*—I believe I

speak the sentiments of the great mass of intelligent citizens soldiers, who are not merely household troops, sir, but who have recently had an opportunity of demonstrating before the world what use they can make of arms in the enemy's country. I speak their sentiments, sir, when I say that the great Kossuth *doctrine of armed non-intervention, is the doctrine and sentiments* of America. Non-intervention for us—non-intervention for all."

To which Kossuth responded:

" The reception I have already experienced relieves me from much anxiety. If the doctrine of non-intervention is understood as you state, then the *generous and efficient aid* of the United States to my country's suffering independence is gained.

He came, then, to secure the " generous and efficient aid of the United States," which was the Kossuth doctrine of non-intervention. It has been our doctrine from the foundation of the government, " to stay at home, and to attend to our own wars—to our own business." This was the non-intervention principle inculcated by the immortal Washington. Kossuth announced in England his object to be to unite England and the United States in the same policy. Was England to yield to us, or we to England? And when he was informed that his doctrine of " armed non-intervention " was the sentiment of " three millions of stalwart Americans," his soul was unburdened, and he proclaimed that he came to seek their " generous and efficient aid."

As to the motive which brought him to this country, he says:

" The motive, citizens, is that your generous act of my liberation has raised the conviction throughout the world, that this generous act of yours is but the manifestation of your resolution to throw

your weight in the balance where the fate of the European continent is to be weighed. You have raised the conviction throughout
the world, that by my liberation, you were willing to say, 'Ye
oppressed nations of old Europe's continent, be of good cheer; the
young giant of America stretches his powerful arm over the waves,
ready to give a brother's hand to your future.' So is your act interpreted throughout the world."

He goes on to say :

"It is hence, that my liberation was cheered from Sweden, down
to Portugal, as a ray of hope. It is hence that even these nations
which most desire my presence in Europe now, have unanimously
told me, hasten on, hasten on, to the great, free, rich and powerful
people of the United States, and bring over its brotherly aid to the
cause of your country, so intimately connected with European liberty."

European liberty, the liberty of Portugal and Sweden,
which countries had cheered him on in the cause of his
country's liberation. He came as the representative of
"European liberty," beseeching our people to stretch
"their powerful arm over the waves," and render "efficient aid" in behalf of those principles with which Portugal and Sweden sympathized. He came as the type
of the social democracy of Germany, of the Red Republicans of France, of the patriots of Italy, who have
exchanged the maxims of absolute monarchies for an
unbounded licentiousness, passing, as is usual, from one
extreme to another. He came as the champion of those
principles which the Germans of Richmond and of
Louisville have here proclaimed, and sought our aid to
re-establish them in Hungary.

Again he said :

"And taking my ground on this principle of union, which I find
lawfully existing, an established constitutional fact, it is not to a

party, but to the united people of the United States, that I confidently address my humble requests for aid 'and protection to oppressed humanity. I will conscientiously respect your laws, but within the limits of your laws I will use every honest exertion to gain your operative sympathy, and your financial, material, and political aid for my country's freedom and independence, and entreat the realization of those hopes which your generosity has raised in me and my people's breasts, and also in the breasts of Europeans oppressed. And, therefore, thirdly, I beg leave frankly to state that my aim is to restore my fatherland to the full enjoyment of this act of declaration of independence, which being the only rightful existing public law of my nation."

There is a law on the statute book, which makes it treason for any man to aid in setting on foot any expedition against a friendly power, and yet Kossuth, notwithstanding his declaration that he would conscientiously respect our laws, came to seek our "*financial, material and political aid.*" He endeavored by his gifted oratorial powers and his persuasive eloquence, to arouse our people up and enlist them in the cause of the unbounded licentiousness of the social democracy of Europe, which has only served to bind the chains of power tighter and to add a century to the enslavement of Europe.

A few days subsequent to his arrival in New York he was invited to review the militia of that city. He appeared before them in Hungarian uniform, and in a speech to them he said:

"I am told that I will have the high honor to review your patriotic militia. Oh, God! how my heart throbs at the idea to see this gallant army enlisted on the soil of freedom against despotism, the world would be free and you the saviors of humanity."

His heart throbbed with joy at the hope that our

militia would array themselves against the fundamental
principles of their country, against the policy of Washington, and in favor of the policy of Louis Kossuth.
His bosom heaved with excitement at the prospect that
his appeals to them in behalf of the down-trodden millions of Europe had enlisted them in the cause of German radicalism, and the socialism of France, and that
henceforth the warning of Washington, to avoid all
entangling alliances, would go unheeded by a people to
whom he had bequeathed this rich heritage of ours.

Not satisfied with these appeals to our sympathies, he
even dared to suggest to us, what policy we should
adopt in our intercourse with a country with whom we
were at peace.   Here is his language :

"Now as to your minister to Vienna, how you can combine in
letting him stay there with your opinion of the cause of Hungary, I
really don't know ; but so much I know, that the present absolutistical atmosphere of Europe, is not very propitious to American
principles. I know a man who could tell some curious things about
this matter. But as to Mr. Hulseman, really I don't believe, that he
would be so ready to leave Washington. He has extremely well
digested the caustic pills, which Mr. Webster has administered to
him so gloriously."

How true are the words, "the absolutistical atmosphere of Europe is not very propitious for American
principles," and how unpropitious for American principles are the "absolutistical" immigrants from Europe !
They have breathed this atmosphere from youth to man-
hood, and come thoroughly imbued with all the principles which Kossuth himself proclaimed ; for in his New
York speech, he stated frankly his object was to perpetuate the Hungarian constitution, which was the "only

rightful existing public law of my nation," which constitution secured to Hungary independence; that is, independence as Europe understood it, for in the same speech he said :

"Hungary is a free and independent kingdom (KINGDOM), having its own self-constituted existence and constitution, and not subject to any other nation and country in the world. The only tie between us (Hungary) and Austria, was that we *we were bound to elect to be our kings the same dynasty which were also the sovereigns of Austria.*"

Here, then, it is perceived that European freedom, in which Portugal and Sweden sympathized, and for which he, as the representative of the millions of Europe who thirsted for liberty, was struggling, consisted simply in the privilege of being compelled (bound is the word) to elect the sovereigns of Austria their king. This is the liberty which he sought to re-establish in Hungary, and which elicited from the German organizations in this country such enthusiastic co-operation. It was not for constitutional liberty, and "natural right and reason," for which he labored so zealously, but for the privilege of being governed by the monarch of another nation.

This is not all. On the 4th of July, 1848, Kossuth presented to the archduke a petition for aid to enable the Hungarians to keep in subjection another people. The Sclavonians had rebelled against the authority of the Magyars, and in their petition to the Emperor of Austria, for protection, they said :

"Emperor, if you reject our prayers, we shall know how to vindicate our liberty with you; and we prefer to die heroically, like a Sclavonian people, rather than to bear such a yoke as is imposed upon us. Emperor, you know that we prefer, if we must choose between them, the knout of the Russians to the insolence of the Magyars."

To which Kossuth, in his petition to the same, of July 4th, 1848, responded thus :

"The Hungarian nation, which, at this time, when almost every throne in Europe is tottering, remains, not only the firmest, but the *only firm prop of the Austrian throne.* This feeling and this experience have led us to request the kind assistance of his highness the Archduke John, with respect to the Illyrian rebellion."

This was the beginning of the struggle which terminated in the subjugation of Hungary, and then Kossuth declared that Hungary, of which he was the dictator, was the only "firm prop of the Austrian throne."

In 1848, he was petitioning for aid to sustain himself in the dictatorship of Hungary, and basing his claim for assistance to subjugate the Sclavonians, upon the ground that Hungary, through him as its dictator, was the only "firm prop of the Austrian throne ;" and in 1851, with that arrogance only becoming to a vanquished despot, he comes to America to solicit aid in re-establishing the "only firm prop of the Austrian throne ;" but he comes not in meekness and in sorrow, but with all the pomp and show of regal splendor, clad in the robes of office, glittering with the emblems of authority, and accompanied by a suite of subordinates. As such he was invited by the American Congress to the Capitol, and welcomed upon the floor of each House of Congress. Before the American Senate he stood as the guest of the nation, not as a war-worn veteran, whose life had been devoted to the cause of constitutional liberty, but as the exiled protector of the Austrian throne, bearing upon his person the insignia of the dictatorship, and the sword dangling at his side.

His career did not stop here. Elated with his success thus far, he proceeded to canvass the whole country, inculcating the principles of European liberty, and sowing broadcast the seed of discord, turbulence, and sedition, and everywhere the German population flocked around him, singing anthems to his praise, and responding to his demands for " material aid," with a liberality far more than justified by their scanty means.

He travelled through the South and the West, peddling his dollar, of which here is a curious specimen :

"HUNGARIAN FUND.—On demand, one year after the establishment, in fact, of the INDEPENDENT HUNGARIAN GOVERNMENT, the holder hereof shall be entitled to ONE DOLLAR, payable at the National Treasury, or at either of its agencies at London or New York, or to exchange the same in sums of fifty dollars or over, for certificates bearing four per cent. interest, payable in ten equal annual installments from one year after said event.

"L. KOSSUTH."

On the 23d June, 1852, Kossuth addressed an assemblage of Germans at the Tabernacle, in the city of New York, after which the following resolutions were adopted :

" *Whereas.* The whig party, in their platform, recently adopted at Baltimore, which has been adopted by their candidates, have declared themselves against participating in the fate of Europe; and, whereas, furthermore, the democratic party in America, which, at least, in their fundamental principles, cherish progress, have not declared themselves against partaking of the European struggle for liberty ! and the policy of intervention may be expected to be adopted by the democratic party as well as by their candidates; therefore,

" *Resolved*, That as American citizens, we will attach ourselves to the democratic party and will devote our strength to having a policy, of intervention in America carried out.

" *Resolved*, That, we expect that the candidate of the democratic party will adopt the pr inciples of this policy, which has been sanctioned by all distinguished statesmen of the party.

" *Resolved*, That we protest against the manner in which, heretofore, the government of the United States has interpreted and applied the policy of neutrality, which is in violation of the spirit of the Constitution of the United States.

" *Resolved*, That we ask that every American citizen, not being attached to the soil, may support the strength of any other people in the sense as the juries have interpreted the principles of the American Constitution, and especially of the policy of neutrality.

" *Resolved*, That we ask that the United States be officially represented by an ambassador to each nation which is battling against monarchism, and has framed its own constitution.

" *Resolved*, That we will unite, hand in hand, with all German-Americans in the Revolutionary Union of Europe for the advancement of the real progressive policy in America and Europe, and that we desire the committee of arrangements of the meeting to frame statutes for the said end, and to do everything necessary for the promotion of the said Revolutionary Union.

" *Resolved*, That we confidently hope that all nations of Europe struggling for liberty, as well as their leaders, according to the principles of solidarity, will consider their end a common one, without interfering with the independence of each nation, and that they rest united in the days of peace and war.

" *Resolved*, That we express our thanks and sympathy to Governor Kossuth, and to the German agitators, for their noble efforts : that we promise them results, and that the Germans of New York and environs will continue to work for the great end of a universal liberation of all nations."

These resolutions contain the principles enunciated

by Kossuth in his speech in the Tabernacle, to give force to which, and to more generally enlist the Germans in their behalf he issued the following secret circular, in which he advises the Germans to assert their political power and influence and to force if possible the democratic and whig parties to acknowledge the justice and necessity of the principles therein set forth.

KOSSUTH'S SECRET CIRCULAR TO THE GERMANS.

"NEW YORK, *June 28th*, 1852.

"SIR: I hope you have already read my German farewell speech, delivered June 23th in the Tabernacle at New York, and also the resolutions of the meeting which were passed subsequently.

"I hope, further, that the impressions which this matter has made *upon both political parties* has not escaped your attention.

"Indeed, it is not easy to be mistaken that the German citizens of America will have the *casting vote* in the coming election, if they are united in a joint direction upon the platform of the principles set forth in the speech mentioned.

"They may *decide* upon the exterior policy of the next adminstration of the United States, and with that upon the triumph or fall of liberty in Europe.

"Never yet were the German citizens of America in this decided position.

"The leaders of the political parties have arrived at the acknowledgment of this power, and they are alarmed, for they know that in the most unfavorable case, the Germans are able to make unsafe, at least, any combination or calculation of the parties.

"Will the German citizens concede this important position, which will not come back in a century?

"I hope God, the Almighty protector of liberty, may prevent it. They are neglecting the moment. Won't they esteem principles higher than names and denominations of parties?

"I hope they will. The position of America is a power—the

3*

liberty of Europe, of Germany, of Hungary, of Italy, depends upon them.

" For God's sake do your best ; that your German fellow citizens occupy this position and ratify the principles put up in said speech, by meetings and resolutions, and declaring the intimated direction as theirs.

" Act quickly. Keep the power of the position uncompromised in your hands, until the one or the other party offer substantial guarantees. This is now of the utmost importance. If I should be so happy as to induce the German citizens in different parts of the United States publicly to approve of my principles and of the intimated direction, thereby furnishing the argument that they would support this policy, this would put me in a position to carry *on efficient negotiations with the parties,* and would enable me to offer such guarantees to them as will answer the principles and sympathies of German hearts.

" God sees my most secret thoughts. He knows it is mere vanity which agitates my heart. No! the consciousness that European liberty depends upon the unanimous support of the German citizens of America, stimulates me in making this communication.

" My requests are as follows :

" 1. Cause a German meeting to be called without delay. The object of it should be to consent which way the German citizens of America should take in the pending Presidential question.

" 2. A committee of influential men—if possible of both parties —should prepare resolutions, among which the following.

" *a.* That the German citizens of ———, who are entitled to vote, approve of the principles laid down in my New York speech of June 23d, and sustain the means and policy which were recommended there ; because they acknowledge them as such that are only and solely fit to promote the true interest of the United States, and of freedom in Europe. On that reason they should govern the conduct of all German citizens.

" *b.* That they request me publicly not to leave the United States without having communicated before the German citizens of ——— *which party* have given the most acceptable assurances, or rather, guarantees, of being resolved to act on this basis in the Presidential question.

" *c.* That they consider especially the repeal, or at least an interpretation of the neutrality laws of 1818, conformable to the principles of the individual rights, guaranteed by the Constitution to the citizens of the United States, as a specially desirable issue.

" *d.* That they request their fellow citizens of other races to unite with them on that high basis of universal liberty, and of the honor and welfare of the United States.

" These proceedings would be of immense importance; open actions and secret intrigues are at work to annihilate this success.

" But the Germans *have become a power;* woe to them if they should neglect this hint of Providence! The movement must be crystallized, that it may not waste it strength. The more it is manifest that I and my policy may rely upon the support of the German citizens, the more I can do for that matter which is so dear also to your hearts.

" In the name of the veneration I entertain for America, in the name of the oppressed nations of Europe, I conjure you to lend us your aid in the direction intimated.

" Let us hear of an activity so ardently longed for.

" With high esteem, fraternal respects, and shaking of hands, your most obedient.

("Signed.)

" L. KOSSUTH.

" N. B.—So far is this confidential, that the letter is not to be given to the public, but is to be used only for private communication.

In his footsteps quickly followed the accomplished Kinkle, delighting audiences with his eloquence and plausible plans for the liberation of the millions of Europe ; and collecting from " the sage inhabitants " of the West, from fifteen to twenty thousand dollars per day either for the purpose of aiding the Revolutionary League in carrying into effect their plans, or for some kindred purpose. And these money orators are aided in their schemes by such appeals as this, issued by the ' Supreme Directory."

"To the Germans in America! The news brought to these shores by each successive steamer from Europe, proves that the hour of *insurrection is near;* therefore, the *refugees must organize and hold themselves in readiness.*

"At a mass-meeting, held Nov. 9, 1853, a commission was elected for the purpose of organization, and that commission, finding unoccupied that difficult position which it was requested to take, now calls upon the German emigration in America to acknowledge them as the centre in all matters regarding that affair.

"The commission has adopted the following platform as the basis of its operations:

"*We recognize the solidarity of all revolutionary interests; our first object being, however, the deliverance of Germany from its political thraldom without our presuming to decide by anticipation other secondary objects. We expect* that the people of Germany will themselves decide upon their future political system, and we-place ourselves at the disposition of the revolutionary government."

* * * * * * *

"To our former revolutionary companions we say, Be prepared! The approaching struggle between liberty and despotism will be severe, but it will be the last; for it will only terminate with the annihilation of one of the two opposing irreconcilable principles."

Add to this the sage reflections of Mazzini. In writing to some friend in this country, probably a member of some one of the Revolutionary Leagues, he said:

"Twenty-four millions of emancipated Italians will be *twenty-four millions of abolitionists* to aid their brethren in America!"

Kossuth sought our aid to re-establish the "only firm prop to the Austrian throne;" and Mazzini offered as a compensation for aid in emancipating Italy, the assistance of "twenty-four millions of Abolitionists," to aid Americans in supporting their Constitution, and to secure the perpetuity of their institutions. The one sought the dictatorship of Hungary, the other the destruction of American institutions. The foreign population afforded them ample material upon which they could operate. From the native population they expected but little. They appealed to the passions, prejudices, and animosities of the foreigner, refreshed his memory with the recollections of his youth, and depicted to him in glowing language the injuries and suffering of his fatherland.

Fatherland! In that single word lie concealed all the hopes of the foreigner. It was the home of his ancestors; in its soil lie buried kindred and friends. He rejoices over its prosperity, and mourns over its adversity.

CHAPTER IV.

REMITTANCES FROM AMERICA.

ONE who had not taken the trouble to ascertain the amount of money remitted from this country, by the foreign population to their friends at home, would be startled at the enormous amount of gold and silver which is, by this means, withdrawn from circulation, and exported to foreign countries. It is impossible to ascertain, with any degree of accuracy, the amount, but the sum known to be remitted annually is very large. The English commissioners of emigration have returned the following sums remitted from America, as having come under their own knowledge:

1848,	. . . .	$2,226,400
1849,	. . . .	2,613,600
1850,	. . . .	4,719,000
1851,	. . . .	4,825,480
1852,	. . . .	5,000,000
		$19,384,480

Whole amount remitted during the years of '48, '49, 50, '51, and '52, which came to the knowledge of the

English commissioners, amounted to $19,384,480. The actual amount must have far exceeded this, for it is presumed that only that portion of the remittances which were intended for England, Scotland, Ireland, and Wales, could come to the knowledge of the English commissioners. The immigration from other countries during these years has exceeded that from England, Scotland, Wales, and Ireland, and the amount of remittances increases in proportion to the immigration; hence, it is fair to infer that the remittances to other European countries equalled that which came to the knowledge of the English commissioners.

The following paragraph from the Cork (Ireland) "Examiner," gives the amount of remittances to Ireland during the years 1853 and '54:

"In 1853, the amount of money sent home for payment of passages, as well as for various other purposes, was £1,439,000; but in 1854, that amount, vast and wonderful as it was, was far exceeded, it having reached £1,720,000, or nearly 300,000 over what it was in the previous year. In the history of the world there is nothing like this amazing proof of the strength and attachment which has ever distinguished and adorned the calumniated Irish race."

Thus it is readily perceived, that the Irish population of this country remitted, during the year 1854, eight millions two hundred and fifty thousand dollars; which amount of money was expended in defraying the expenses of immigrants to this country. It is more than probable that every family in Ireland has a representative in this country, who hoards up, from his scanty earnings, enough to pay the cost of transporta-

tion of the remaining members of the family. This
Irish paper asserts one other fact, viz.: these remittances
evidence the "strength and attachment" of the Irish of
this country to the land of their birth.

We expend annually millions of dollars in maintaining foreign paupers, and a large amount in prosecuting
foreign criminals; we feed the hungry, and clothe the
naked; we grant them the rights of citizenship, and
confer upon them honors and emoluments, and yet they
are not satisfied; we must even pay the cost of transportation. What a privilege, indeed, we are thus permitted to enjoy! We are not only permitted to invite
" our company and entertain them," but must even pay
the cost of conveyance. What a pleasure! And all
this charity and benevolence on our part but proves the
"strength and attachment" of this calumniated race.
Eight millions of dollars annually expended in Irish
remittances—enough to float our entire navy! In the
history of the world there is nothing like this amazing
generosity—yet they are not satisfied. They live upon
our substance, yet they want our political blessings, and
seek to model them after their own crude ideas of
liberty, freedom, and equality. They sit at our table
and around our hearthstones, and still they grumble.
Their appetite cannot be satiated, their wants cannot be
supplied, nor can their wishes be gratified; yet our
doors are open to them. How long must we bear all
these grievances? "Self-preservation is the first law of
nature." The time is not far distant when we shall
even be compelled to forsake the " Old Homestead,"
and leave it to the Vandals. How soon it will become
desolate. In view of this result, let us unite upon the

common platform of self-preservation, and pledge " our lives, our fortunes, and our sacred honors," to protect our rights, to perpetuate our institutions, and to preserve our nationality.

CHAPTER V.

SHIPMENT OF PAUPERS AND CRIMINALS.

THERE can exist no doubt that the states of continental Europe ship to this country many of their paupers and convicts; many have been sent here at the expense of their own government, who had become nuisances to their own country. Many were inmates of penitentiaries and prison houses, and have been sent here as a measure of safety to their own country.

If there be any doubt as to the correctness of this statement, it is only necessary to examine the past history of the country. General Smith, while mayor of the city of Baltimore, transmitted to the President of the United States a German newspaper, in which this notice was given:

"A transport of inmates from the house of correction in Gotha will sail for Bremen, under escort of a police officer, and thence to America, either to New York or Baltimore."

This same gentleman, subsequently, informed the President of the arrival off the ship, and that "the irons were knocked off the limbs of the convicts only when they came in sight of our coast."

The " Montreal Herald " of Dec. 22, 1840, contains the report of the " Immigrant Committee of Montreal," and the speech of Dr. Rolph, " the accredited immigrant agent of the government of Great Britain," in which he says that the government of Great Britain had expended, during the nine preceding months, $17,000 in that city, in forwarding immigrant paupers. Of the total number of immigrants to Canada during those months (23,160), but 7,013 were able to defray their own expenses; and of the paupers, 8,625 came (were sent) to the United States. England has had in operation, for twenty years past, a system of emigration, through which means she has gotten rid of the large portion of " her lower orders " (as she terms them), and within a few years back, several other of the European governments have adopted the plan of relieving themselves of the burdens of pauperism and crime, by transporting the paupers and convicts to this country, at the expense of their respective governments. The press of England, and in some of the continental states, has frequently urged upon their governments the necessity of home depletion by emigration.

Captain Marryatt, the English traveller, who visited this country, and published a journal of his travels, in describing the scenes he witnessed on board of the ship in which he came over, uses this language: " What cargoes of crime, folly, and recklessness do we yearly ship off to America." These were the cargoes which England was shipping under the auspices of her " Emigrant Aid Societies," of which there were several accredited agents on this continent, and that portion which was sent to Canada was ultimately re-shipped to this country. It was the duty of the accredited agent at Montreal to forward or to aid all immigrants to the place of their destination, and in the report, before alluded to, it is distinctly stated, that the number, 7,013 who were able to defray their travelling expenses, proceeded to Upper Canada, and that of the remaining number, none of whom were able to pay their own expenses, 8,625, came (were sent) to the United States. It will occur to the reader as a very remarkable circumstance, that all who were not paupers should " proceed to Upper Canada," and much the larger portion of the others should " proceed to the United States." It is true that England desired to settle Upper Canada, and she took good care to have an " accredited agent at Montreal," and he a physician, who should cause only those able to pay their expenses to proceed to Canada. This is the system which has been, for twenty years, pursued by England, by way of depleting herself, and burdening the United States with the care of her paupers and criminals.

The English press of the present day teem with laudations upon this policy, and urge the government to extend her operations, enlarge the sphere of action of the " emigrant aid societies," to appropriate money to defray the expenses, and to aid this most charitable and benevolent English institution to the fullest extent of her powers. Other countries have followed in the wake of England, and now scarcely a day passes, but that the journals announce the arrival of an immigrant ship, at some one of the seaboard cities, laden with the maimed and diseased carcasses of European paupers and criminals, which have been transported hither by

European authorities, either in obedience to their strict and rigid sanitary regulations, or as a measure of personal safety and security.

During the fall of 1854, a vessel landed in New York one hundred and fifty paupers, and fifteen convicts, wearing, as the badges of their conviction, chains upon their limbs; and a few months subsequently another vessel, freighted with a similar cargo, was wrecked on Sable Island, from whence her passengers were carried to Halifax, and from Halifax were brought to New York, by way of Boston. By an affidavit made by one of these passengers, it appeared that they were natives of Switzerland, who, being unable to support themselves at home, were sent hither, at the expense of the municipality to which they belonged.

The following is the affidavit:

" City and County of New York, *ss:* We, the undersigned, being duly sworn, do depose and say out, that we and our families, whose number is correctly taken down opposite to our names, on the foot of this affidavit, are natives of Switzerland; that they were poor in their own country, and could not support themselves there any longer; that therefore the mayor of their village has paid their passage money direct to New York, and that therefore their passage money has not been paid by these deponents : that they embarked at Antwerp, on board the ship Arcadia, which vessel was intended for New York, but wrecked at Sable Island; that they sailed from Boston on board the passenger steamboat State of Maine, and arrived in the port of New York on board the said steamer, on the 2d day of January, 1855; that they are now quite destitute, and without any means for support, except from commissioners of emigration, and further they do not say.

[Here follow signatures.]

" Sworn before me, this tenth day of January, 1855.

"EDWARD CASSERLY,

"*Commissioner of Deeds.*"

About the same time, the Sardinian government shipped on board a "national vessel (the Degennes man of war), thirty-four convicts—not convicts for political offences, but convicts for crime of the most dangerous description." The arrival of this ship at New York called forth the following letter from Mayor Wood of that city, to the President of the United States:

MAYOR'S OFFICE, NEW YORK, *January* 2, 1855.

"HIS EXCELLENCY FRANKLIN PIERCE, PRESIDENT OF THE U. S.

"DEAR SIR: There can be no doubt that, for many years, this port has been made a sort of penal colony for felons and paupers, by the local authorities of several of the continental European nations. The desperate character of a portion of the people arriving here from those countries, together with the increase of crime and misery among that class of our population, with other facts before us, prove, conclusively, that such is the case.

"It is unnecessary to refer to the gross wrong thus perpetrated upon this city. It requires from me no allusion to the jeopardy of our lives and property from this cause. Men who by a long career of crime and destitution, have learned to recognize no laws, either civil or natural, cannot fail to produce feelings of terror at their approach.

"The inherent right of every community to protect itself from dangers arising from such immigration, cannot be questioned. New York has submitted to it long enough. The disease and pauperism arriving here almost daily, from abroad, is, of itself, a sufficient evil; but when to it is added crime, we must be permitted to remonstrate. We ask the interference of the General Government. As it is its duty to protect us from foreign aggression, with ball and cannon, so is it its duty to protect us against an enemy more insidious and destructive, though coming in another form.

"I call your attention to this subject, hoping I will receive from you that action which its very great importance to the whole country demands. I am very truly yours, &c.,

"FERNANDO WOOD, *Mayor*."

The petty kingdom of Wurtemburg has been in the habit, for some years past, of shipping to this country its pauper and infirm criminal population to save the expense of maintaining them at home.

In some instances, it appears that the Commissioners of Emigration in New York, thought that the yoke imposed upon them pressed a little too heavily, and thereupon ventured to return certain of the most indifferent specimens of Wurtemburg humanity to their own country.

Wurtemburg had paid the passage of these lazars to America for the purpose of getting rid of them, and while it is congratulating itself on the " artful dodge," lo and behold they re-appear, as tattered and torn as when they went away. The Commissioners of Emigration having sent them back, paternal Wurtemburg lashes itself into a passion, and straightway launches against the American authorities the following manifesto:

" *Whereas*, it has repeatedly occurred that German emigrants to America, and among them natives of Wurtemburg, who desired to return home on account of sickness or incapacity to labor, have been forwarded to this country by the German Emigration Society; and

" *Whereas*, it is desirable that those who have once emigrated to America, and especially those who have been transported thither at the expense of the states or the communes, and are unable, whether or not it be from any fault of their own, to earn their subsistence, should not return here to be a burden to the state or the commune, (*which in that case will have defrayed the expenses of their journey in vain ;*) and

" *Whereas*, the American authorities are scarcely authorized to send back those who, having once been admitted to the country, cannot earn their subsistence in America ; and

"*Whereas*, it is much less the business of the German Emigration Society of New York to promote the return of such individuals; therefore,

"*Resolved*, That necessary steps are to be taken to prevent their transportation back to this country."

Wurtemburg thinks that those who have been transported hither "at the expense of the state or the commune, ... should not be permitted to return there to be a burden to the state or communes." And that we, because Wurtemburg has succeeded in discharging a cargo of paupers and criminals at one of our ports, should not re-ship the same to the kingdom of Wurtemburg.

The following is an extract from a message of Mayor Wood of New York, to the city authorities, in relation to the shipment of paupers to that city.

"It has long been the practice of many governments on the continent of Europe, to get rid of convicts and paupers, by sending them to this country, and most generally to this port. The increase of crime here can be traced to this cause rather than to defect in the criminal laws or their administration. An examination of the criminal and pauper records, shows conclusively that it is but a small proportion of these unfortunates who are natives of this country. One of the very heaviest burdens we bear is the support of these people, even when considering the direct cost; but when estimating the evil influences upon society, and the contaminating effect upon all who come within the range of their depraved minds, it becomes a matter exceedingly serious, and demanding immediate and complete eradication. I know of no subject of more importance; certainly, we have the power to protect this city against the landing of so vile an addition to our population; the health as well as the life and property of the people for whom you legislate, requires some action at your hands. I am confident the general government will listen to any representations from you relating to it, and interpose its national authority in our behalf.

" On the 2nd instant, I made this grievance the subject of an official communication to the President of the United States."

Additional proof from the correspondence of the U. S. consuls, on file in the State Department at Washington:

" MR. HARRISON TO MR. LIVINGSTON:

" CONSULATE OF THE UNITED STATES, KINGSTON, JAMAICA, *June* 28*th*, 1851.

" SIR : I do myself the honor to inform you that I was called upon yesterday by most of the masters and supercargoes of American vessels now in this port, who complained of a law which obliges all foreign vessels under one hundred tons to take a pauper."

" CONSULATE OF THE UNITED STATES, DISTRICT OF KINGSTON-UPON-HULL, LEEDS,
" *Aug.* 30*th*, 1836.

" SIR: . . . The officers of customs are well aware that paupers do proceed to the United States and Canada; and it has been admitted by the owners of several vessels trading there, that their passages are paid by the overseers of the parishes to which they belong. . . .

" ALBERT DARY,
" *Consul U. S. A.*"

" U. S. A. CONSULATE, BREMEN, *Sept.* 8*th*, 1836.

" SIR : . . . Families, almoners, and civil authorities, in order to get rid of a burdensome fellow, or troublesome subject, pay what is necessary for such a person to cross the Atlantic. . . . . .

" H. W. BOHNEL,
" *Consul.*"

" CONSULATE U. S. A., LEIPSIC, *March* 8*th*, 1837.

" SIR : . . . Not only paupers, but even criminals are transported from the interior of this country to sea-ports, in order to be embarked for the United States. . . . .

" F. LIST,
" *Consul.*"

4

" U. S. Consulate, Switzerland, *March* 27, 1856.

"Sir: . . . Four authorities and cantonial governments have been in the habit of sending their paupers to the United States, merely securing their passage to New York."

During the 2d Session of the 28th Congress, Mr. Berrien made a report in relation to the shipment of paupers and criminals to this country, accompanied with the testimony from which the following is extracted. Henry Lampaiter, jun., testified that he knew of

" The instances of two persons—one named Christopher Brown, and one named Henry Knapp." And that he had "learned from a woman who accompanied them, that they both had been sent to this country from a house of correction in Brunswick."

William Wardenburg said :

"He knows that criminals and paupers have been sent to this country from Europe; knows that paupers from the almshouses of Germany were sent here by the government."

Abraham Cuyk said :

" It is well known, any of the German kingdoms are very willing to empty prisons, and give them five or ten dollars to get rid of them ; and certainly the Bremen merchants do not care how they load their vessels, if they only get paid for it, if they are murderers, burglars, or paupers."

Moses Catzenstein :

"Knows a criminal who was transported to this country ; cause, for drunkenness and robbery."

Samuel I. Robbins testified as follows :

"I believe that foreign convicts have been introduced into this country. This belief is formed upon inquiries made."

George Henry Poulsen swore thus :

" I know of many instances where convicts have been pardoned and sent to this country at the expense of the government by which they were pardoned. Ten or twelve such cases have come to my knowledge."

Lawrence Herbert deposed as follows :

" It is my opinion and belief, founded upon my observation, that foreign criminals have been introduced into the United States from some of the states of Germany, by authority of governments or cities."

Lenon Carolier said :

"That there is no doubt of the introduction into the United States of a large number of vagabonds and criminals coming from foreign countries.".

Moreau Forrest, marshal for the Maryland district, said :

" The captain of a ship, whose name was Edwards, told me that he had received from the corporate authorities of Kingston one doubloon for each of the steerage passengers."

Henry Caton deposed that he

" Has known persons in Bavaria sent by government to this country for state offences."

Samuel Cohen swore as follows :

"It is a practice in Germany for the government to give passports to criminals and paupers, directing that they shall proceed direct to America."

Sufficient has been adduced to prove that there is now, and has been for a number of years, in operation a regular system of shipping criminals and paupers from foreign countries to this. The seaboard towns have remonstrated against this practice, and appealed to the state and national governments for relief, yet none has been granted. They still groan under the burden of this evil, which increases every year, and which is not only a tax upon their pecuniary resources, but the source of much the larger portion of the distress, suffering, pauperism, and crime with which all our seaport towns are afflicted.

CHAPTER VI.

LABOR.

THE statistics of the occupations of the inhabitants of the United States are very meagre and unsatisfactory. The census of 1850 fails, in this respect, in several important particulars. The number of persons, both male and female, pursuing the various trades and occupations is given, but the nativities are omitted.

To institute a comparison between the native and foreign population, to ascertain the relative proportion of each class pursuing any particular occupation, and to deduce from such a comparison the advantages and disadvantages of immigration to the various trades and professions, it is essentially necessary to have authentic statistics concerning the same. In these investigations, it has been, and will continue to be, the aim of the author to base the facts upon, or deduce them from, official and authentic data.

The only statistics in the census of 1850 in relation to this subject is a table showing the occupation of passengers arriving in the years 1845, 1847, and 1852, from which, and from the annual report of the Secretary of State for 1854 is compiled the following table :

Occupation.	1845.	1847.	1852.	1854.
Laborers	18,656	37,571	82,571	82,420
Servants	1,659	3,198	948	3,310
Not stated, or no } occupation . . }	52,768	115,167	209,131	234,396

The occupations of labors, service, and " not stated,"
or no occupation, have been selected, because they com-
prise the whole number of immigrants who are brought
in direct competition with American labor.

The following table exhibits the number of each of
these occupations, and the arrivals for the years stated :

Year.	Arrivals.	Servants.	Laborers.	No occupation.
1845	119,884	1,659	18,656	52,768
1847	239,480	3,198	37,571	115,167
1852	398,470	948	82,571	209,151
1854	460,474	3,310	82,420	234,396

Half of the arrivals in these four years had no occupation, one-fifth were laborers, and only three-tenths
were mechanics, farmers, and tradesmen. Seven-tenths
of the arrivals in the years enumerated were laborers
or had no occupation, and it is more than probable that
seven-tenths of the whole number of arrivals or immigrants are laborers or have no occupation. The effect
of this immense influx of the laboring and "no occupation" immigrants, will inevitably depreciate the value
of American labor. The price of labor depends upon
the demand and supply, and it is indisputably true that
for the last few years the supply has increased in a
greater ratio than the demand, and consequently the
value has diminished, and a large accession has been
made to the " no occupation" class of population ; or

many, even among the native, who earn their livelihood by the "sweat of their brow," have been compelled to toil for barely sufficient to supply the actual necessaries of life. The meeting of foreigners which took place in the city of New York during the winter of 1855, which was addressed by Roedel, originated in the fact that in that great city the supply of labor was far greater than the demand.

This influx of labor from abroad, which is so antagonistic to the interests of the American laborer, is another circumstance which is likely to hasten that conflict of races which is daily threatened and from which so much danger is to be apprehended.

The following table, compiled from the census, exhibits the number of American laborers of the States enumerated as compared with the number of foreign laborers who arrived during the year 1854. The native laborers of the male sex only are given; and much the larger proportion of female laborers, both native and foreign, are enumerated under the heads of "servants" and "no occupation," therefore the comparisons instituted in the table below approach very nearly to absolute accuracy:

State.	Laborers.	Emigrant laborers of 1854.
Maine	21,000	82,420
New Hampshire .	13,662	"
Vermont	21,993	"
Massachusetts . .	52,661	"
New York . . .	174,867	"
New Jersey . . .	36,361	"
Pennsylvania . .	148,967	"
Maryland	28,908	

State.	Laborers.	Emigrant Laborers of 1854.
Virginia	46,989	82,420
Ohio	86,868	"
North Carolina . .	28,143	"
Indiana	28,165	"
Illinois	27,910	"

The immigrant laborers of 1854 exceed the number of native laborers in each State, with but three exceptions (New York, Pennsylvania, and Ohio). And the aggregate immigrant laborers of 1852 and 1854 exceed the native in each of those three States. The whole number of male laborers (slaves are not included) in the United States in 1850, as shown by the census, was 909,786; and the whole number of immigrant laborers for the years 1845, 1847, 1852, and 1854 was 221,218.

Add to the laboring population of any State the immigrant laborers of any one of the years since 1850, or of any one of the five immediately preceding that date, and then conjecture the effect upon the value of labor in such State. For instance, in 1850 the native male laborers of Maine numbered 21,000, each one of whom commanded a certain price, and it is to be presumed the supply was equal to the demand. Say each received one dollar per day, and the number of working days in a year was three hundred. This would give $300 dollars per year per laborer, and the aggregate cost of American labor, in Maine, for the year 1850, would be $6,300,000. Add to the American laborers the immigrant laborers of 1854, the aggregate of the two classes will be 103,420. Labor is worth but $6,300,000 in Maine, which would yield an average yearly income of $69,91 to each of the laborers of both classes, or 23⅓ cents per day. A similar calculation might be made in reference to the other States. In those States where the native laborers number less than in the State of Maine, the reduction would be much greater, and in those States where the native laborers exceed in number those of Maine, the reduction would not be so great. The instance cited is sufficient to demonstrate the practical effect of immigration upon the value of American labor. The calculation has been based upon the presumption that the per diem of the laborers remain the same, thus omitting entirely the effect of competition, the tendency of which is to depreciate the value of labor.

In view of the consideration here presented, is not immigration an evil? To the capitalist it is not. It is the ally of the money power of the country, and this money power is being constantly exerted to depreciate the value of labor and of property in which it seeks investments, and the depreciation of the value of any description of property indirectly lessens the value of labor. The capitalists of this country are the allies of Great Britain, and the two in conjunction rule the money market of the world. American labor is the great antagonist to this money power, and it behoves the government of the United States to foster and nourish it, for it is the great bulwark of freedom, and the foster-mother of liberty. It is now being crippled by immigration, and by the same the money power is being made more potential. The augmentation of the money power will more closely unite America and England, and oppress the laboring classes, and especially the American laborers; because immigration both directly and indirectly contributes to this power, in the first instance, by creating a demand for capital and money, and secondly, by depreciating the value of American labor.

--- ◆◆◆ ---

CHAPTER VII.

LAW OF INCREASE.

THE matter of increase of foreigners by birth, is well worth a careful examination.

The production or increase by birth is in ratio to the number of females who have reached the age of production, and not to the whole population; because in the latter event men, children, and women who have passed beyond the age of production, would be reckoned in the calculation, and, consequently, the comparison thus instituted between the foreign and native population would be incorrect; because the number of productive females is much larger among the whole native population, than the number of productive females is among the foreign population, yet the proportion of productive females among the foreign female population is much greater than it is among the native, and as the number of children must depend upon the number of productive females, it must follow that the increase must bear a ratio to the productive females.

Foreigners generally intermarry with each other, so far as has been observed. It is very rare that a native marries a foreigner or vice versa; these few exceptions

do not affect the general rule.   Every day the instances
of intermarriage between natives and foreigners become
less frequent, because the two classes of population are
constantly becoming more exclusive.   With the Irish,
this rule is almost invariable, and but very few exceptions occur among the Germans.

Among the immigrant population there is a much
larger number of males than females, and it is undoubt-
edly true, that the marriages among the immigrants
equal the number of productive females, and it is a
very rare occurrence to find an immigrant female who
has arrived at the proper age, and not grown too old,
unproductive.   It is then established,

1. That the increase must be in ratio to the productive females.

2. That marriages among the immigrants are equal
in number to the productive females.

To determine the ratio of increase between the native
and foreign, it must first be ascertained what proportion
of females are productive in both classes of population,
and what is the relative proportion of productive
females of the two classes.   In 1847, the immigrant
males were 139,491, and females 99,328, being in the
ratio of 583 males and 417 females, per 1,000 of both
sexes.   All females of twenty years of age, and not
exceeding forty, are regarded as productive.   This is
the rule, though there are many exceptions to it, but
the exceptions will not affect the result of any calculation based upon the rule, because there are as many
productive females not included within the rule as there
are unproductive included within it.   Among those
who came in 1847, the females between twenty and

forty years old were 49 per cent. of their own sex, and
203 per 1000 of both sexes, and among all the white
natives in 1840 (according to the census), the females of
this age were only 143 per 1000. This would give the
foreigners an advantage of 41.9 per cent. in this respect,
that is, the per cent. of productive females among the
immigrants is 41.9 per cent. greater than the per cent.
of productive females among the native population. It
must, then, follow, that if the marriages among the two
kinds are relatively equal, or if the excess is in favor of
the immigrant population, the rate of increase among
the latter is far greater than it is among the native. It
remains now to ascertain the proportion or per cent. of
marriages among the immigrants and natives, respectively, to the whole immigrant and native population,
and also the relative proportion of the marriages among
the two. On page 121 of De Bow's compendium of the
census of 1850, the following statistics may be found :
" In Massachusetts and in Boston, where the means of
making the comparisons exist, there is a much greater
proportion both of births and marriages to the population of each kind, among the foreign than among the
native," within the years 1849, 1850, and 1851.

The following table compiled from these statistics
shows the difference between the marriages among each
kind, in proportion to the population respectively, in
every 10,000 of each kind.

Massachusetts.	Population.	No. of Marriages.	Marriages in every 10,000
Native . . .	830,066	18,286	220
Foreign . . .	164,448	7,414	450

During these three years there were 220 marriages in

every 10,000 native Americans, and in every 10,000 foreigners there were 450 marriages. The per cent. of marriages among the native population is 2.02, and among the immigrant is 4.05, which is 104.5 per cent. excess over native ratio.

To test the accuracy of this calculation, it is but necessary to institute the same comparison between the kinds of population of the city of Boston, thus:

Boston.	Population.	No. of Marriages.	Marriages in every 10,000.
Native	75,322	4,678	541
Foreign	63,466	5,073	799

The per cent. of marriages among the native population, is 5.40, and among the foreign, 7.90, which is an excess of 84.8 per cent. of foreign over native per cent. " The productive females in Massachusetts in 1840 among the native, were 163 per 1,000 of all, and in the United States, 143 per 1,000; yet, the productive ratio of the immigrants is 26.3, above that of the people of the States." The excess of foreign ratio, in regard to marriages, above the native is much less in the city of Boston than in the State of Massachusetts, taken as a whole, but it is sufficient in either instance, to demonstrate the fact, that the proportion of marriages among the foreign, is far greater than among an equal number of native, and equally clearly is it demonstrated that the productive ratio of females among the foreign is much greater than among an equal number of native; the inference then is clearly deducible, that the ratio of birth is far greater among the foreign than the native, for it has been shown before, that the births must be

in ratio to the productive females, but it is best not
to rely upon an inference, the fact is not only deduceable
but easily demonstrated by the following tabular view,
for the years 1849, '50, '51 :

Massachusetts.	Population.	Births.	Births in every 10,000.
Native . .	830,066	47,982	578
Foreign . .	164,448	24,523	1,491

There were 578 births in every ten thousand natives,
and 1,491 among every ten thousand emigrants, nearly
three foreign to one native.

The same is true of Boston, as is shown by the following table.

Boston.	Population.	Births.	Births in every 10,000.
Native . .	75,322	7,278	966
Foreign . .	63,466	13,032	2,053

These facts are admitted in a pamphlet recently published by A. O. P. Nicholson, public printer, of which
Louis Schade (mark the name) is the author.   This
pamphlet is entitled " The Immigration into the United
States of America," and from which the following
extract is taken :

"The State of Massachusetts had, in 1850, 830,066 native, and
164,448 foreign born inhabitants, or one foreigner to five natives.
The marriages were, during the years of 1849 to 1851, Americans,
18,286, or 220 in 10,000 of their own race ; foreigners, 7,440, or 450
in 10,000.   This is 104.5 per cent. of foreign over native ratio.
The births were in Massachusetts in the three years 1849, '50, and
'51, of American parents, 47,982, or 578 in 10,000 of their own
race ; foreign, 24,523, or 1491 in 10,000 of their own race.   In
Boston there were, American 7,378, or 966 in 10,000 ; foreign

13,032, or 2,053 in 10,000 of their own race. Of the 32,000 born in Massachusetts in 1854, 16,470 were of American parentage, while some 14,000 were of parents one or both foreigners; and the increase from foreign parents was more than twice what it was from native parents. *At the same rate shortly we shall have more children born in Massachusetts from foreigners than from natives ;* for in five years the American births have not increased 1,000, while the *foreign have increased more than* 5,000. In Suffolk county already the births in foreign families are more than twice as numerous as in American, being 3,735, in the former, and 1,737 in the latter. Of the parents of Boston children, in 1854, the largest number was from Ireland, 2,824 fathers and 2,957 mothers, while there were but 410 fathers and 524 mothers natives of the city, and 533 fathers and 475 mothers natives of Massachusetts, out of Boston, or of other States. Cambridge had born of foreign parents 422 children to 208 Americans ; Fall River, 223 to 88 ; Lawrence, 322 to 146 ; Lowell, 596 to 427 ; Roxbury, 383 to 168; Salem, 344 to 120 ; Taunton, 221 to 142; and Worcester, 421 foreign to 320 American."

Again :

" If we take the census returns for 1850, we will find the number of births to be 548,835, and the number of deaths 271,890—confining ourselves to the white and free colored population. The difference, being 276,945, was the increase of population for 1850 from excess of births over deaths."

The immigration in 1850 amounted to 279,980, which exceeded the increase of the whole population of this country for that year by births 3,035 ; thus, by the showing of Mr. Schade and A. O. P. Nicholson, editors of the "Washington Union," the immigration is greater than the natural increase of the nation. Since 1850, the relative increase of immigration above the natural increase of the nation, has greatly augmented, and as this increases, the evil of immigration increases, because the foreign population, if we add to its increase by birth, its increase by immigration will double relatively in half the time that the native will, and of course its power will increase at the same ratio.

It is useless to pursue this investigation or examination of statistics any further. Every issue arising under the law of increase between the native and foreign population is demonstrated to be in favor of the foreign. The facts cannot be contradicted, and if the same comparisons were instituted between the foreign and native population of any other State or city, the result would be similar. Massachusetts and Boston have only been selected because the census statistics were more complete, and these two had been selected by its author as illustrations.

The facts demonstrated are,

1. That a greater tendency to marriage exists among the immigrants than among the natives.

2. That there is a more rapid production among the immigrant than among the native.

To the statesman and patriot these are not unimportant facts. The rapid propagation of the immigrant races tends, in a great measure, to prevent the assimilation of those races with the American people, and the more nearly the two classes of population approach to an equality of number, the more danger there will arise of an absorption, either partial or complete, of the American character by the immigrant population. Another effect of this rapid propagation among the foreign, is to preserve and perpetuate the habits, customs, peculiarities, and distinctive characteristics of the immigrants. It has been shown in another part of this treatise, that two distinct nationalities cannot exist together harmoniously under the same jurisdiction, and certainly, every circumstance which seems likely to widen the breach between the foreigners and the natives, and which seems calculated to perpetuate and extend the influence of foreign peculiarities, should demand the serious consideration of every patriot and statesman.

In three years a foreign population numbering 63,466, gave birth to 13,032 children. At that rate of increase, and at the present rate of immigration, the foreign element will, at no very distant day, infuse itself into every department of the government, and warp and bias its direction. These are no idle speculations based upon inferences, and ocasional observations, but the legitimate deductions from the past histories of nations and of governments.

In 1850 (DeBow's Compendium) there were 2,244,602 foreigners residing in this country, and the descendants of foreigners are variously estimated from 700,000, up to 2,000,000. The descendants of the immigrants of the present day are far inferior to those of the past half century. When immigration was but a few thousand annually, they rapidly assimiliated with the American character, became absorbed, losing all their distinctive peculiarities, but the absorbent has long since ceased to perform its wonted task, because it was over-tasked.

CHAPTER VIII.

THE following letters from General Washington, written during the revolutionary war, and which may be found in *Sparks's Publication of the Washington Papers*, are commended to the calm perusal of the reader.

The closing sentence of General Washington's letter to Gouverneur Morris, dated July 24th, 1778, contains a *sentiment*, expressed in relation to the military services of foreigners, which came from the bottom of the patriotic heart of the Father of his country, and which *puts to flight* the arguments of all the demagogues of the present day on this question.

"*I do most devoutly wish*," says Washington, "*that we had not a single foreigner among us*, except the Marquis de Lafayette, who acts upon different principles from those which govern the rest." Was not Wasington sincere in that "*wish*," thus "devoutly" expressed?— Was he not qualified, to judge of their merits and demerits, their aims and purposes? If not qualified *who was?*

"These men," says Washington, in his first letter, "have no attachment to the country, further than interest binds them."

"It is," says he, "by the zeal and activity of our own

90

people that the *cause* must be supported, and not by a few *hungry adventurers.*"

Did General Washington utter falsehoods, when he thus expressed himself? Are his opinions entitled to no weight? Is his testimony of no value in the decision of this question? Here are the letters:

TO RICHARD HENRY LEE.

" MORRISTOWN, *May* 17, 1777.

"DEAR SIR: I take the liberty to ask you what Congress expects I am to do with the many foreigners they have at different times promoted to the rank of field officers, and, by their last resolve, two to that of colonel? These men have no attachment to the country, further than interest binds them. Our officers think it extremely hard, after they have toiled in the service, and have sustained many losses, to have strangers put over them, whose merits, perhaps, are not equal to their own, but whose effrontery will take no denial. *
* * It is by the zeal and activity of our own people that the cause must be supported, and not by a few hungry adventurers. * *

" I am, &c.,

" G. WASHINGTON."

TO THE SAME.

" MIDDLEBANK, *June* 1, 1777.

" You will, before this can reach you, have seen Monsieur Decoudray; what his real expectations were, I do not know, but I fear, if his appointment is equal to what I have been told is his expectation, it will be attended with unhappy consequences, to say nothing of the policy of intrusting a department, on the execution of which the salvation of the army depends, to a foreigner, who has no other tie to bind him to the interests of the country than honor. I would beg leave to observe, that by putting Mr. D. at the head of the artillery, you will lose a very valuable officer in General Knox, who is a man of great military standing, sound judgment, and clear conception, who will resign if any one is put over him.

* * * * * * *

"I am, &c., G. WASHINGTON."

TO GOUVERNEUR MORRIS, ESQ.

"WHITE PLAINS, *July* 24, 1778.

" DEAR SIR: The design of this is to touch cursorily upon a subject of very great importance to the well-being of these States; much more so than will appear at first view. I mean the appointment of so many *foreigners* to office of high rank and trust in our service.

" The lavish manner in which rank has hitherto been bestowed on these gentlemen will certainly be productive of one or the other of these two evils—either to make us despicable in the eyes of Europe, or become a means of pouring them in upon us like a torrent, and adding to our present burden.

" But it is neither the expense nor trouble of them I most dread; there is an evil more extensive in its nature and fatal in its consequences to be apprehended—and that is, the driving all our own officers out of the service, and throwing not only our own army, but our military councils, entirely into the hands of *foreigners*.

" The officers, my dear sir, on whom you must depend for the defence of this cause, distinguished by length of service and military merit, will not submit much, if any longer, to the *unnatural* promotion of men over them, who have nothing more than a little plausibility, unbounded pride and ambition, and a perseverance in the application, to support their pretensions, not to be resisted but by uncommon firmness; men who, in the first instance, tell you they wish for nothing more than the honor of serving in so glorious a cause as volunteers; the next day solicit rank without pay; the day following, want money advanced to them; and in the course of a week, want further promotion. The expediency and policy of the measure remain to be considered, and whether it is consistent with justice or prudence to promote these military fortune-hunters, at the hazard of our army.

" Baron Steuben, I now find, is also wanting to quit his inspectorship, for a command in the line. This will be productive of much discontent. In a word, although I think the baron an excellent officer, *I do most devoutly wish that we had not a single foreigner among us*, except the Marquis de Lafayette, who acts upon very different principles from those which govern the rest.   Adieu.

"I am, most sincerely, yours,

'G. WASHINGTON."

TO JOHN QUINCY ADAMS.

"MOUNT VERNON, *Jan.* 20, 1799.

"SIR: I have been honored with a letter from you, dated at Berlin on the 29th of October last, covering one from a namesake of mine, and who may very probably be a distant relation, as our families were from the same country—mine earlier than his—two brothers migrating during the Commonwealth of England, or rather during the troubles of Charles I.   Not knowing through what other medium to address him, I take the liberty of sending my answer to his request under cover to you.

"You know, my good sir, that it is not the policy of this country to employ aliens, where it can be well avoided, either in the military or civil walks of life; but for want of provident care and foresight, they will find themselves (indeed they now begin to feel it) under the necessity of resorting to foreign aid for skillful men in the engineering and artillery corps.   If my namesake is well instructed in either of these branches of military science, which, by the by, is hardly to be expected from his age, there would be no doubt of his favorable reception—without which I think it would be deceptious to encourage hopes of employment in the army of the United States; for there is a species of self-importance in all foreign officers that cannot be gratified without doing injustice to meritorious characters among our own countrymen, who conceive, and justly, where there is no preponderancy of experience or merit, that they are entitled to the occupancy of all offices in the gift of the government."—Vol. ii., pp. 391–2.

TO JOHN ADAMS, VICE PRESIDENT OF THE UNITED STATES.

"SATURDAY, *November* 27, 1794.

"DEAR SIR: I have not been able to give the papers herewith enclosed more than a hasty reading, returning them without delay, that you may offer the perusal of them to whomsoever you may think proper. The picture drawn in them of the Genevese is really interesting and affecting. The proposition of transplanting the members entire of the university of that place to America, with the requisition of means to establish the same, and to be accompanied by considerable emigration, is important, requiring more consideration than under the circumstances of the moment I am able to bestow upon it.

" That a national university is a thing to be desired, has always been my decided opinion; and the appropriation of ground and funds for it in the Federal City has long been contemplated and talked of; but how far matured, or how far the transporting an entire seminary of foreigners, who may not understand the language, can be assimilated thereto, is more than I am prepared to give an opinion upon, or, indeed, how far funds in either case are attainable.

" My opinion, with respect to emigration [immigration is meant, of course], is, that except of useful mechanics and some particular descriptions of men or professions, there is no need of encouragement; while the policy of its taking place in a body (I mean the settling of them in a body) may be much questioned; for by so doing they retain the language, habits, and principles, good or bad, which they bring with them; whereas, by an intermixture with our people, they or their descendants get assimilated to our customs, measures, and laws—in a word, soon become our people."— Vol. ii., pp. 1, 2.

In an order to the Massachusetts Bay forces, signed by Horatio Gates, Adjutant General, the following sentence is found:

" You are not to enlist any person who is not an AMERICAN born, unless such person has a wife and family, and is a settled resident in this country."

In another, issued from Cambridge Head Quarters, July 7, 1775, signed by Fox, Adjutant for the Day, in speaking of the sentries, the following is found:

"No man shall be appointed to those stations who is not a NATIVE of the country."

Again, at Valley Forge, March 17th, 1778, in giving a description of the kind of men to be enlisted, Washington said:

"They must be AMERICAN born."

In a letter addressed to a person applying for office, dated Jan. 20th, 1790, he said:

"It does not accord with the policy of this government to bestow offices, civil or military, upon foreigners, to the exclusion of our own citizens."

In a letter to Sir John St. Clair, England, he said:

"I have no intention to invite immigrants, even if there are no restrictive acts against it: I am opposed to it altogether."

These were the opinions of the immortal Washington. But he did not stop with them. In his farewell address, he said:

"Against the insidious wiles of foreign influence—I conjure you to believe me, fellow-citizens—the jealousy of a free people ought to be constantly awake; since history and experience prove, that foreign influence is one of the most baneful foes of a republican government."

To this add the following of Jefferson:

"I hope we may find some means, in future, of shielding ourselves from foreign influence, political, commercial, or in whatever form it may be attempted. I can scarcely withhold myself from joining in the wish of Silas Dean—' that there were an ocean of fire between this and the Old World.' "

And others :

"Foreign influence to America, is like the Grecian Horse to Troy; it conceals an enemy in the heart. We cannot be too careful to exclude its entrance."—*Madison.*

"It is time that we should become a little more Americanized, and instead of feeding the paupers and laborers of England, feed our own; or else, in a short time, by our present policy, we should be paupers ourselves."—*Jackson.*

"They make our elections a curse instead of a blessing."—*Martin Van Buren.*

"Lord preserve our country from all foreign influence."—*Last Prayer of Gen. Jackson.*

"The people of the United States, may they remember, that to preserve their liberties, they must do their own voting and their own fighting."—*Harrison.*

OTHER TESTIMONY.

The Continental Congress passed the following resolution :

" *Resolved*, That it is inconsistent with the interest of the United States, to appoint any person not a natural born citizen thereof, to the office of minister, charge d'affaires, consul, vice-consul, or to any civil department, to a foreign country."

The following order was issued during the administration of the elder Adams :

"For cavalry, the regulations restrict the recruiting officers to engage none except native."

John ·Adams, in a letter to Christopher Gadsden, said :

"Americans will find that their own experience will coincide with the experience of all other countries; and foreigners must be received with caution, or they will destroy all confidence in government."

Mr. Jefferson, in a letter to Mr. Jay, writing from France, said :

"Native citizens, on several valuable accounts, are preferable to aliens, or citizens alien born. . . . . To avail ourselves of native citizens, it appears to me advisable to declare by standing law, that no person, but a native citizen, shall be capable of the office of consul."

Henry Lee, in his oration on the death of Washington, delivered, Dec. 20, 1799, said :

"Shut up every avenue to foreign influence."

The following was adopted by the same Virginia Legislature which passed the celebrated Virginia resolutions of 1798, and the report of 1799—the great platform of the Southern States Rights party. These resolutions passed December 24th, 1798, and the following twenty-six days after :

"Preamble and resolutions passed by the Legislature of Virginia, on the 16th day of January, 1799 :

"That the General Assembly, nevertheless concurring in the opinion with the Legislature of Massachusetts, that every constitu-

5

tional barrier should be opposed to the introduction of foreigners into our National Council:

"*Resolved*, That the Constitution ought to be so amended that no foreigner who shall not have acquired rights under the Constitution and laws at the time of making this amendment, shall not thereafter be eligible to the office of Senator or Representative in the Congress of the United States, nor to any office in the Judiciary or Executive Department.

"Agreed to by the Senate, January 16, 1799."

At a later date, impressed with the truth of the facts we have mentioned, Daniel Webster, with the sententious brevity peculiar to the man, recorded it as his firm conviction:

"That there is an imperative necessity for reforming the naturalization laws of the United States."

The private correspondence of Mr. Clay, recently published, shows that, in the opinion of himself and leading friends, his defeat was owing to the foreign vote which was arrayed against them. It will be seen, from the following extracts, that the apprehensions entertained by the Americans, regarding the influence of foreign Catholics, is nothing new. In a letter, dated Buffalo, November 11, 1844, Mr. Fillmore writes to Mr. Clay as follows:

"The abolitionists and foreign Catholics have defeated us in this State. I will not trust myself to speak of the vile hypocrisy of the leading abolitionists now. Doubtless many acted honorably, but ignorantly in what they did. But it is clear that Birney and his associates sold themselves to locofocoism, and they will, doubtless, receive their reward.

"Our opponents, by *pointing to the Native Americans and to Mr.*

Frelinghuysen, drove the foreign Catholics from us and defeated us in this State."

In a letter addressed to Mr. Clay, by Theodore Frelinghuysen, dated New York, November 9, occurs the following paragraph:

"More than three thousand, it is confidently said, have been naturalized in this city alone, since the 1st of October! *It is an alarming fact, that this foreign vote has decided the great questions of American policy, and contracted a nation's gratitude.*"

Extract from Washington's will:

" It has always been a source of serious regret with me, to see the youth of these United States sent to foreign countries for the purposes of education, often before their minds were formed, or they had imbibed any adequate ideas of the happiness of their own; contracting too frequently not only habits of extravagance and dissipation, but principles unfriendly to republican government, and to the true and genuine liberties of mankind, which thereafter are rarely overcome."

In a letter to Nathaniel Macon, Speaker of the House of Representatives, Mr. Jefferson said:

" A very early recommendation has been given to the Postmaster-General, to employ *no foreigner* or revolutionary tory in any of his offices."

In 1797, Jefferson drew up a petition for the citizens of Albemarle, Amherst, Fluvanna, and Goochland counties, Virginia, which is found among his writings, and published in the " Baltimore Sun." It seems that Jefferson thought that none but Americans should be placed on juries. He says:

" And your petitioners further submit to the wisdom of two Houses of Assembly, whether the safety of the citizens of this Commonwealth, in their persons, their property, their laws and government, does not require that capacity to act in the important office of a juror, grand or petit, civil or criminal, should be restricted in future to the citizens of the United States, or such as were citizens at the date of the treaty of peace which closed our Revolutionary War, and whether ignorance of our laws and natural partiality to the countries of their birth, are not reasonable causes for declaring this to be one of the rights incommunicable in future to our adopted citizens ?"

The following is an extract from an oration delivered by James Buchanan, on July 4th, 1815 :

" Above all, we ought to drive from our shores foreign influence, and cherish exclusively American feeling."

From a report of W. H. Crawford, Secretary of War under Mr. Madison, the following extract is taken :

" It will redound more to the national honor to incorporate, by a humane and benevolent policy, the natives of our forests in the great American family, than to receive with open arms the fugitives of the Old World, whether the flight has been the effect of their crimes or virtues."

Judge Woodward, in the Pennsylvania Convention of 1837, in reply to some strictures upon him, for having introduced a resolution, instructing a committee to inquire in the expediency of amending the constitution of the State, so as to prohibit foreigners from voting after a certain period, said :

" I believe, that if the time has not yet come, it will speedily come, when it will be indispensably necessary, either for this body, or some other body of this State, or of the United States, to inquire

whether it is not right to put some plan in execution, by which foreigners should be prevented from controlling our elections and brow-
beating our American citizens."

For this act, the foreigners never forgot him, and
when Judge Woodward was urged for the vacancy on
the supreme bench, the following petition of foreigners
was sent to the President:

" TO PRESIDENT POLK.

" PHILADELPHIA, *Dec.* 18*th*, 1845.

" SIR : We are naturalized citizens, and members of the Democratic party, who, having heard with extreme surprise, that Geo. W.
Woodward has been urged upon you as a person qualified to fill the
vacancy upon the bench of the Supreme Court, beg leave most earnestly to remonstrate against any such appointment. In the convention to amend the constitution of Pennsylvania, this gentleman proposed so to amend it, ' as to prevent any foreigner, who might
arrive in this State after the 4th of July, 1841, from acquiring the
right to vote or hold office in this Commonwealth.' Such doctrines
might have been suited to the days of the elder Adams, but were
considered by every Democrat as entirely at war with the principles
of the great Democratic party. These principles were luminously
expounded in the resolutions of the Baltimore convention, and upon
that faith we urged and advocated your election with all our zeal
and strength. We do sincerely, therefore, trust, that they will be
fully carried out in relation to this great judicial question. There
is an intense excitement among our naturalized citizens, which nothing could restrain, if such a nomination were to be made. We,
therefore, protest most solemnly against George W. Woodward."

While the bill was pending in the House of Representatives, to re-charter the United States Bank in 1816
(Annals of Congress, 1st session, 1815-16),

"Mr. Randolph moved to add the word *native* in the clause which limits the choice of directors to 'citizens of the United States; which motion was agreed to without debate—ayes, 68."

Subsequently, on a motion to amend the bill in a similar manner, in regard to the directors of the branch banks, Mr. Randolph said :

"It was indisputably true, that it was to our system of naturalization laws the United States owed the spirit of faction by which they had been torn for the last twenty years, and along with it, the war out of which the country had just emerged. He spoke from the information of statesmen, inferior to none in this or any other country, that the system of granting protection to foreign seamen, was one of the chief causes of the war with Great Britain, which system had grown out of our naturalization laws. Much had been said, and he dared to say much more would be now said, and much more be written on this subject, for it was a melancholy truth, that the press was in the hands of those very people who had long taken upon them to dictate to the American people, and to tell them who ought to be their President, who their Vice-President, and who their Representatives, and to direct them in their most essential concerns. He was aware, therefore, that the press would be at work, and that much would be said and much printed about what he was now saying ; but that had no terror for him. How long the country would endure this foreign yoke, in its most odious and disgusting form, he could not tell ; but this he would say, that if we were to be dictated to, and ruled by foreigners, he would much rather be ruled by a British Parliament than by British subjects here. Should he be told that those men fought in the war of the Revolution, he would answer, that those who did so, were not included by him in the class he adverted to. That was a civil war, and they and we were, at its commencement, alike British subjects. Native Britons, therefore, then taking arms on our side, gave them the same rights as those who were born in this country, and his motion could be easily modified, so as to provide for any that might be of that description ; but no such modification, he was sure, would be found necessary, for this plain reason. Where were the soldiers of the Revolution who were not natives? They were either already retired, or else retiring to that great reckoning where discounts were not allowed. If the honorable gentleman would point his finger to any such kind of person now living, he would agree to his being made an exception to the amendment. It was time," Mr. R. said, " that the American people should have a character of their own; and where would they find it? In New England and Virginia only, because they were a homogeneous race, a peculiar people.

" They never yet appointed foreigners to sit in the House for them, or to fill their high offices. In both States this was their policy; it was not found in, nor was it owing to, their paper constitutions; but what was better, it was interwoven in the frame of their thoughts and sentiments, in their steady habits, in their principles from the cradle—a much more solid security than could be found in any abracadabra, which constitution-mongers could scrawl upon paper. It might be indiscreet in him to say it, for, to say the truth, he had as little of that rascally virtue, prudence, he apprehended, as any man, and could as little conceal what he felt, as affect what he did not feel. He knew it was not the way for him to conciliate the manufacturing body, yet, he would say, that he wished with all his heart, that his boot-maker, his hatter, and other manufacturers, would rather stay in Great Britain, under their own laws, than come here to make laws for us, and leave it to us to import our covering. We must have our clothing home-made," said he, " but I would much rather have my workmen home-made, and import my clothing. Was it best," he demanded, " to have our own unpolluted republic peopled with our own pure native republicans, or erect another Sheffield, another Manchester, and another Birmingham, upon the banks of the Schuylkill, the Delaware, and the Brandywine, or have a host of Luddites amongst us, wretches from whom every vestige of the human creation seemed to be effaced? Would they wish to have their election on that floor decided by a rabble? What," he asked, " was the cause of the ruin of old Rome? Why, their opening their gates, and letting in the rabble of the whole world to be her legislators. If," said he, " you wish to preserve among your fellow-citizens that exalted sense of freedom which gave birth to the

Revolution—if you wish to keep alive among them the spirit of '76—you must endeavor to stop this flood of foreign emigration. You must teach the people of Europe that if they do come here, all they must hope to receive, is protection: but that they must have no share in the government. From such men, a temporary party may receive precarious aid, but the country cannot be safe, nor the people happy, where they are introduced into government, or meddle with public concerns in any great degree!"

So far as regards the associations of past history, the American people have as much cause to hate foreigners, *as a class*, as to love them. Foreign soldiers were hired in Germany, by England, in the Revolution, for the purpose of being sent here to crush us. And they *were* sent, and their devastations and freebooting conduct became so proverbial, that, to this day, their character is immortalized in the name of that insect—the Hessian fly—whose ravages are so destructive to the farmers' hopes. So far, then, as regards the past, while we ever should, as the nation does, cherish a feeling of gratitude for individual instances of devotion to the cause in the war of the Revolution, by foreigners, yet, as a class, the Americans have as much cause to dislike them, as they have to love them.

But to come down to the late war with Mexico. It is a favorite illustration to compare Arnold with Lafayette, and thence argue that all foreigners are Lafayettes, and that as Arnold was a native traitor, it is probable most natives are traitors.

It may refresh the patriotism of such traducers of their countrymen, and advocates of aliens, to read the following description of an American and foreign soldier, on the same battle-field:

" AN AMERICAN SOLDIER.—Most providentially, at that moment, Taylor arrived with Davis's (Hon. Jefferson Davis), Mississippi Riflemen and May's Dragoons. The former barely stopped an instant, for the men to fill their canteens, then hastened to the field. Boiling with rage, Davis called on the Indiana Volunteers to form 'behind that wall,' pointing to his men, and advance against their enemy. Their Colonel (Bowles), the tears streaming down his face, finding all his appeals fruitless, seized a musket, and joined the Mississippians as a private. Time could not be lost; Ampudia was close upon them. Davis formed and advanced, with steady tread, against a body of more than five times his strength. A rain of balls poured upon the Mississippians, but no man pulled a trigger till sure of his mark. Then those deadly rifles blazed, and stunned the Mexican advance. A ravine separated them from the enemy. Davis gave the word, and, with a cheer, down they rushed, and up the other side; then, forming hastily, with one awful volley they scattered the Mexican head, and drove them back to cover."

" A BATTALION OF IRISH DESERTERS CAPTURED.—Notwithstanding the parley, one Mexican battery continued its fire upon our troops. This was the 18 and 24-pounder battery of the battalion of San Patricio, composed of Irishmen, deserters from our ranks, and commanded by an Irishman named Riley."

We would recommend the toadies to tell the War Department that an Irishman was as brave a man, and as good a friend to America as a Mississippian!

As a further proof of the conduct of this Irish battalion, we quote from the speech of Mr. Butler, a Democratic Senator from South Carolina, on the Homestead Bill, which was to give land to foreigners. He said:

" A man may come reeking from the jails and poor-houses of Europe; I will go further, and say, that the deserters upon your field of battle may come—men who fought against those who won your territories—can come and take land without having sworn the oath of allegiance. Yes, sir, the very deserters upon the plains of

Cherubusco, who shot down your regiments, might come and take possession of your lands. . . . . . . These deserters were foreigners, who shot down my own regiment," (meaning the Palmetto regiment).

Hear, also, what General Shields, an Irishman himself, says, in reference to this San Patricio regiment:

"The command which I had the honor to accompany that day (the day of the battle of Cherubusco), composed of the gallant Palmetto regiment, the New York regiment, the United States Marines, and also the brigade led by the present President of the United States, were attacked (and suffered very severely by that attack), not only by Mexicans, but by a body of deserters, led by a very notorious character, whose name was Riley. I am not sure whether he was born in Ireland or in this country, but he was either an Irishman, or the son of an Irishman."

This is good democratic Irish testimony. But General Shields says still more, viz.: that they gave him the most trouble, "for they were men who fought most bravely." They fought bravely against the Americans, from whose ranks they had deserted. Furthermore, says General S.: "My aid-de-camp went round after the battle (where these *Irish traitors* had been captured), by my orders, and ascertained their names, and the countries of their birth, and found that they were *Germans*, *Irish*, and one or two *Englishmen*." This is the language of General Shields, himself an Irishman, testifying to the nativity of these deserters!

What paupers do to the economy.

CHAPTER IX.

EVILS OF IMMIGRATION.

AMONG the evils incident to immigration, crime and pauperism are not the least important. That much of the crime and pauperism in this country is due to this source, no one will deny. To ascertain the relative proportion of these two evils among the immigrant and native population, there cannot be a more impartial course pursued, than to institute a strict and rigid comparison between the two, and to make from such comparison, such deductions as are logical and evident to every unbiased and unprejudiced mind. Upon this basis, the following investigation will be made:

FOREIGN AND NATIVE PAUPERISM.

The census of 1850 shows that, during the year ending June 30, 1850, the number of persons who received " the benefit of the public funds of the different States," was 134,972; of this number there were 68,538 of foreign birth, and 66,434 native Americans. The total cost of maintenance was $2,954,806, averaging $21 90 per individual, making the total cost of foreign paupers $1,501,882. The number of foreign paupers exceed the native 2,104. From an examination of these statistics it is seen, that the number of foreign and native paupers maintained at public expense, is about equal; but it must be borne in mind, that the native population of the United States far exceeds the foreign; and, to correctly ascertain the comparative contribution to pauperism, we must compare the native and foreign paupers with the native and foreign population. Thus:

	Population.	Paupers.	Proportion pauperism.
Native population	21,031,569	66,434	1 to 317
Foreign population	2,240,535	68,538	1 to 32

One in every 32 foreigners is a pauper; whereas, but one in 317 Americans is a pauper; then it follows that the proportion of native and foreign pauperism is one to ten. These calculations are based upon the census of 1850, and show conclusively that the source of pauperism in this country is immigration. This conclusion is confirmed by an examination of the pauper statistics of those countries from whence come the immigrants. The proportion of pauperism to the population of the European countries, varies from 25 to 15 per cent. In the Netherlands, in 1847, one-fifth of the population were paupers; in Great Britain and Wales, in 1848, one in every eight persons was a pauper, and when these facts are taken in connection with the policy adopted by foreign countries, of shipping to this country their paupers, it is not at all remarkable that the proportion of paupers among the immigrants should be so large. Immigration is indiscriminate, consequently, it is not surprising that the ratio of pauperism to the foreign population is so great. The cause of immigration to this country, to a very great extent, is pauperism abroad ; and pauperism here is the consequence of indiscriminate immigration.

In the foregoing, the statistics of the census of 1850 have merely been considered, which only show the number of paupers, both native and foreign, maintained at public expense. It is a well-known fact that a large proportion is dependent upon private charities. There is hardly a family or housekeeper throughout the land, upon whose charities there is not at least one pauper dependent ; besides, there are many benevolent institutions which maintain by far the largest proportion of paupers. Yet the census returns are sufficiently full and accurate to serve as a basis upon which to estimate the relative proportion of native and foreign pauperism. That has been done, and the proportion is as one to ten —one native to ten foreigners.

Since 1850, immigration has vastly increased, and with it its attendant evils ; and though there are no official estimates of pauperism since that period, there exist sufficient data upon which to venture a calculation.

In the State of New York, during the year 1853, there were maintained 130,027 paupers, at a total cost of $1,009,747 65, at an average of $37 86 per individual. Adopting the ratio of native and foreign pauperism (ten foreigners to one native), and it will appear that this State, during the year 1853, maintained 117,025 foreign paupers, at a total cost of $898,777 89, nearly one-sixth of the entire revenue for the whole State, for one year. During the year ending June 30,

1850, this State maintained 40,580 foreign paupers; in 1853, 130,027—a three-fold increase.

During the year 1854, this State maintained 137,347 paupers, of which, adopting the same ratio, 123,613 were foreigners, at a total cost of $1,008,714 32.

During the year 1855, there were maintained 204,161, of which 119,607 were foreigners, at a total cost far exceeding the previous year.

The Report of the Secretary of the State of New York, which was communicated to the Legislature in January last, in speaking of the subject of pauperism, says:

" The report dwells in forcible language upon the necessity that exists of devising some means by which to meet and lessen the growing evil of pauperism. A reform is deemed necessary in the manner in which provisions are supplied to the poor-houses—many a superintendent being now the merchant or farmer who furnishes the supplies, for which he makes his own charges. Some systematic action is also recommended, by which the labor of paupers can be made profitable. The instance of Rhode Island is cited, where the annual earnings of each pauper was $16 37, while in this State the earnings averaged $3 15. Had the averages been equal, this State would have saved $120,000. Attention is called to the rapid increase of pauperism—the number in 1855 having exceeded the preceding year by 70,000, and the expense by over a million. The census statistics between 1831 and 1851, show the increase of population in twenty years to be sixty-one per cent., and the increase of pauperism *seven hundred and six per cent.*

" In 1831, there was one pauper to every one hundred and twenty-three persons; in 1841, one to every thirty-nine; and this year *one to every seventeen.* The same ratio, continued fifteen years longer, will leave one pauper to every five persons; that is, every five persons in the State must support one pauper. Fifteen years compose a short interval for this State to pass over, and it is worth the while of its citizens to contemplate their condition when every fifth man will be a pauper. When the vote of one-fourth of this State is cast by paupers, and most of them foreign paupers, the ballot box will become the object of contempt. The report considers that the unchecked migration of foreigners is the chief cause of the increase in pauperism, and urges that while it is the duty of the State to take care of its poor, it is a question whether New York should be made the poor-house of Europe, or be taxed to lighten the taxation in foreign countries.

" Under these views, the report urges some action of the Legislature, if any is practicable, by which the tide of pauper and criminal immigration can be checked, and the commonwealth relieved from so unnecessary and heavy a burden, without awaiting the tardy, uncertain action of Congress. This, however, it is thought, would only effect a partial remedy ; as under our liberal laws, the legitimate immigration would still be enormous; and as most of the immigrants exhaust their means in reaching this continent, are unacquainted with our customs, many with our language, and are generally ignorant and degraded, they are unfit for employment, and rear their children as paupers for the State to support. The report therefore deems it essential that more efficient public means of educating those who are to be incorporated into the body politic, in common and religious education, should be adopted by the State. Instead of permitting the children of paupers to be gathered up by the police and crowded by multitudes into our houses of correction and refuge, to learn those vices that lead to poverty, they should be placed under a disciplinary system, and paternal benevolent influences.

" The development of the resources of a State, the expansion of its commerce and the growth of its population, do not advance it one step toward greatness, if vice, and ignorance, and poverty, outstrip them all in progress. Beside, there is a connection between the moral condition and political well-being of a government or commonwealth—so intimate that they cannot be separated. They *must* move on together."

The report is signed by the Secretary of State, the Hon. Joel T. Headley.

The aggregate of the amount expended for the support of foreign paupers during the years 1853, '54, and '55, is $2,916,206 53.

In Massachusetts, during 1853, there were maintained by the State 11,874 foreign paupers. For the year ending June 30, 1850, the number was 9,427; increase, 2,627. During 1853, there arrived in this State, from foreign countries, 1,135 foreign paupers—that is, persons who were actually paupers at the time of their arrival, and are likely to continue so as long as the State of Massachusetts provides for their maintenance.

During the year 1854, 809 foreign paupers arrived in this State.

In ten years, the State of Massachusetts had on charge 119,623 paupers; of this number 90,834 were foreigners.

The State authorities, in their recent report, state that 222,905 persons had been practically relieved or supported, of whom 89,250 had no legal residence in the Commonwealth. The whole cost for relieving and supporting paupers, during ten years (including the interest on almshouses) was four millions one hundred and seventeen thousand two hundred and fifty-one dollars and sixty-three cents; and much the largest portion of this enormous amount has been expended to defray the expenses of foreign paupers.

During the month of November, 1855, the city of New York maintained 5,076 foreign paupers, at the City Dispensary, besides the inmates of the various hospitals, alms-houses, and other charitable institutions.

In the Philadelphia Alms House, during the month of December, 1854, there were

Americans, ...	914
Foreigners, ...	2,407

Same month, 1855,

Americans, ...	688
Foreigners, ...	1,382

The Report of the Superintendent of the Louisville Dispensary, for two months, as published in the "Louisville Journal," gives as the number of patients gratuitously treated at the Dispensary, the following:

Ireland, ...	801
Germany, ...	141
England, ...	11
Scotland, ...	1
Total Foreigners, , . . .	954
Americans, ...	70
Total, ...	1,024

The "Journal" says:

"This disproportion of foreigners to Americans, who are recipients of our public and private charities, exists in all the statistics which have been collected in regard to our charitable institutions. In this instance, out of 1,024 persons gratuitously furnished with medicines and medical attendance in the Dispensary for the western district of our city, more than nine-tenths were of foreign birth.

"It will be recollected that during the last winter soup-houses were established in different parts of our city for the poor, and our various benevolent societies were actively engaged in alleviating the wants of the distressed. Doubtless, if the nativities of the reci-

pients of the assistance from these good Samaritan societies had
been ascertained, it would be seen that the proportion of foreigners
and natives does not differ from that reported by the officers of the
Dispensary.

"All the public and private charities will continue to be sustained. We wish to see them nobly and energetically carried out,
but it is certainly arrant ingratitude on the part of the organs of the
foreign party in Louisville to be continually abusing the native-born
citizens, and endeavoring to render the foreign population discon-
tented and turbulent, in the face of such facts. They show that
there is some good in Louisville, and that foreigners are not so
unkindly treated as the Sag-Nicht papers would fain represent.
The Native Americans of this city have been branded by the anti-
American press throughout the country as 'murderers,' 'thieves,'
and almost demons. Will these foreign organs, who have been so
prompt to abuse the native-born citizens, give them credit for their
unpretending and freely accorded charities toward the foreign
population?"

The patients treated during October and November
1855, at the Louisville Dispensary, were Americans 70,
foreigners 954.

During the month of November 1855, there were
lodges furnished at public expense, at Newark, New
Jersey, Americans 36, foreigners 262.

From the 1st of January to the 1st of October, nine
months, says the "Chambersburg Transcript," there were
entertained in the poor-house in Franklin county, Pa., a
total of wayfaring paupers, amounting to 552.

Americans, ...	30
Foreigners, ...	522

In the twelfth ward, Philadelphia, during the year,
the total number accommodated with lodgings amounted
to 1,822, of which 1,253 were foreigners.

In the city of New Orleans, for the year 1853, there
were admitted into Charity Hospital 13,759 paupers, of
which 12,333 were of foreign birth, and 1,534 natives.
For the year ending June 30, 1850, there were but 423
for the entire State of Louisiana. The increase is startling, and almost incredible.

During the year 1854 the number admitted was 13,192, of which 11,606 were foreigners.

The following extract from the letter of ex-Senator Clemens, illustrates the excess of foreign pauperism over the native:

"By reference to the annual report of the governors of the Alms House, I find that there were in the N. Y. Alms House during the year 1853, 2,198 inmates—of these only 535 were natives, and 1,663 foreigners, supported at the expense of the city. And now I propose to use on our side the argument of our opponents that there are only 3,000,000 foreigners to 20,000,000 natives. According to that ratio there ought to be about seven natives to one foreigner in the Alms House, whereas we find more than three foreigners to one native. No wonder that a people who are taxed to support such a body of paupers should be the first to set about devising means to get rid of them. Let us pursue the record—the Bellevue Hospital, in the same city, there 702 were Americans—4,134 foreigners; now the proportion rises to nearly six to one. There were of out-door poor—that is persons who had some place to sleep, but nothing to eat and nothing to make a fire—967 native adults, and 1,044 children—3,131 foreign adults, 5,229 foreign children, born of foreign parents. This number were relieved during the year with money. Of those relieved with fuel there were 1,248 adult Americans, and 1,801 children—10,355 adult foreigners, and 17,857 children. But the record is not yet complete—let us turn to the statistics of crime. In the city prisons there were during the year 6,102 Americans—22,229 foreigners. I pass on to an abode even more gloomy than that of the prison cell, and call your attention to those whom God in his wisdom has seen fit to deprive of the light of reason. In the lunatic asylum there were admitted from the year 1847 to 1853, 779 Americans—2,381 foreigners. For the year 1853 there were 94 Americans, 393 foreigners.

"These tables might be made more complete by adding organ-grinders, strolling mendicants, and professional beggars; but of these I have no reliable data, and therefore pass them with the single remark that I have never seen a native American who belonged to either class. These figures are far more conclusive than any language could be to prove the necessity of arresting the tide of immigration. Let every American impress them deeply on his memory. 42,369 foreign paupers and invalids; 2,381 lunatics, and 22,229 criminals taxing the industry, and blighting the prosperity of a single city. In that list of crimes is murder, rape, arson, robbery, perjury, and everything which is damning to the character of the individual, and everything which is dangerous to society. In our section we see but little of the evils of immigration, comparatively few among us, and those are generally of the best classes of their countrymen. It is not as a State that we suffer most, but as an integral part of the Republic. The crime, vice, disease, destitution, and beggary which flow in with every tide of immigration afflicts us but little; it is through their political action—in their capacity of voters—that the curse extends itself to us. When thousands upon thousands are carried to the polls and made to vote in favor of any man, or any party, for a shilling, corrupting the ballot-box, and rendering liberty insecure, then we suffer—then the law of self-preservation gives us a right, and makes it a duty to interpose. With such dangers thickening around us, the memorable order of Gen. Washington, should be upon every man's lips—" Put none but Americans on guard to-night." In time of peace your public officers are your sentinels. Put none on guard whose bosoms do not swell with exulting pride at the mention of Bunker Hill, Monmouth, of Saratoga, or of Yorktown. Put none on guard whose national traditions are not confined to our own commonwealth. Put none on guard who can dwell by the hour on the eloquence of Daniel O'Connel, but have never heard the name of Patrick Henry. Put none on guard who turn with indifference from the story of Niagara and New Orleans, to boast of Marengo, Leipsic, and Waterloo. They do not love your land as you do—they will not watch over it with the same absorbing interest. Oppression, not choice, has brought him here, and though he may feel a certain amount of gratitude for the shelter he has found, he still looks back to the green fields of his childhood—he remembers every stone upon the highways—he reads the history of his native land, and partakes in the pride of its great events—in his heart of hearts he feels that there is his home, and there his holiest affections are garnered up. Fear, necessity, common sense, may keep him here, but he loves not the land of the stranger—cares nothing for its former glories—sheds no tear over its former disasters.

" With what reverence can the German regard the name of Washington when he remembers that his pathway to freedom was strewn with the dead bodies of mercenaries? What exultation can the Briton feel in the fame of Jackson when he remembers that it was won by trampling the lion banner in the dust? It is not in human nature that they should feel as we do, and we are false to ourselves, when we put them in power or give them the direction of the law."

The ratio of foreign and native pauperism has been estimated to be in 1850, one native to ten foreigners. The additional statistics of 1853 augment this proportion, and show a much larger proportion of foreign pauperism.

So far, then, as the comparison instituted between the two classes of population, foreign and native, in regard to pauperism, is concerned, the conclusion is inevitable that there is a necessity for a reformation in the naturalization laws. Pauperism is an evil, a curse, a blight, and immigration is its principal source.

FOREIGN AND NATIVE CRIME.

To continue the comparison between the foreign and native population, which has been commenced, the investigation of the subject of crime comes next in order.

The census of 1850 shows that the whole number of persons convicted of crime in the United States, during the year ending June 30, 1850, was 27,000, of which 13,000 were of native, and 14,000 of foreign birth. The foreign exceed the native, 1,000. The relative proportion of foreign and native crime can be determined by comparing these statistics respectively with the foreign and native population, thus :

	Population.	Criminals.	Proportion of crime.
Native population	21,031,569	13,000	1 to 1619
Foreign population	2,240,535	14,000	1 to 154

One out of every 154 foreigners is a criminal, and but one in every 1,619 Americans. The proportion of native and foreign crime, then, is as 1 to 10—one American to ten foreigners.

But another view may be taken of this subject, and in doing so it will be necessary to again call attention to the number of criminals who were convicted by the courts of several States in 1850. In Connecticut, the whole number of convictions was 850 ; and of these, 545 were natives, and 305 foreigners. In Illinois, the whole number convicted was 316 ; and of these, 127 were natives, and 189 foreigners. In Maine, the whole number convicted, 744; and of these, 284 were natives, and 460 foreigners. In Massachusetts, the whole number convicted was 7,250; and of these, 3,336 were natives, and 3,884 foreigners. In Missouri, there were 908 convictions; and of these, 242 were natives, and 666 foreigners. In New York, the number of convictions was 10,279; and of these, 3,962 were natives, and 6,317 foreigners. In Pennsylvania, the number of convictions, 857; and of these, 594 were natives, and 293 foreigners. In Vermont, the number convicted, 79; of whom 34 were natives, and 45 foreigners.

By a table published in the Compendium of the Seventh Census, giving the number of convicts in the prisons and penitentiaries of the several States, out of every ten thousand of the population, the proportion of natives and foreigners in the number is as follows:

	Foreign.		Native.			Foreign.		Native.
In Maine	5	to	1	In Vermont	8	to	1
In Kentucky	6	to	1	In South Carolina	28	to	1
In Mississippi	5	to	1	In Alabama	50	to	1
In New York	3	to	1	In Georgia	6	to	1
In Tennessee	15	to	2	In Indiana	4	to	1

But says the Hon. James Cooper, in a speech delivered in the U. S. Senate, during the 2nd session of the 33rd Congress:

"It is in convictions for capital offences that the proportion of foreign and native-born becomes startling. It is true, we have found no extended data from which to make the comparison. But out of two hundred and twenty convictions which took place, in about eighteen months, in seven States—viz., New York, Pennsylvania, Missouri, Louisiana, New Jersey, Massachusetts, and Maryland—there were 139 foreigners to 82 natives. But our wonder at the magnitude of the proportion of foreigners to natives vanishes, when we recollect that hundreds and thousands of convicts, from European work-houses and prisons, are annually landed on our shores. Trained to crime at home, and sent hither because their presence endangers the peace and security of society in their native country, these men arrive here, in many instances, direct from prison, and consequently destitute of means of support. To obtain it, they betake themselves to their old courses; and not only do they commit crimes themselves, but lead those with whom they become acquainted on their voyage, and who are equally needy, into their perpetration."

To correctly appreciate these statistics, it must be borne in mind that the negro population has been included in the native.

If the comparison had been instituted between the native white population and the foreign, which is also white, thus representing the American and European nations, the relative proportion of crime among the two classes would have been greater, and when the fact is taken into consideration, that only the white native and the immigrant or European population are entitled to or ever exercise the rights of citizenship—which is the only just political view of the question, for it is the political power and influence of foreigners which we seek to counteract and destroy—the comparison thus instituted between the two classes of white people would be more just and appropriate, and would more correctly exhibit the evil and danger attendant upon indiscriminate immigration, to the institutions, safety, and welfare of our common country.

The above calculations are based upon the census of 1850. In Massachusetts, in 1851, there were confined in the various jails and houses of correction, 1,832 natives, and 2,615 foreigners; in 1853, 2,117 natives, and 3,142 foreigners. In these three years, the increase of native prisoners was 265; of *foreign*, 527—thus showing the relative proportion of increase to be one native to two foreigners; yet the native population of the State is six times as great as the foreign. Of the number committed to jail in the State of Rhode Island, during the year 1853, 65 were natives, and 256 foreigners. In the State of New York, during the year 1851, there were convicted and sentenced to the penitentiary 700 persons, of which 300 were of foreign birth, and 403 natives. The native population of the State was 5 1-7 times greater than the *foreign*, yet the number of native

convicts was only 1 1-3 times as many as the *foreign.*
In the Louisiana penitentiary, during the year 1853,
there were 283 convicts, of which 109 were of foreign
birth, and 174 natives. The native population is 5 2-3
times as great as the foreign, yet the number of native
convicts is only 1 1-2 times greater than the *foreign.*

From the American Almanac for 1855, the following statistics of conviction are obtained for the year
1854.

State.	No. of convictions.	Native.	Foreign.	State.	No. of convictions.	Native.	Foreign.
Rhode Island	174	132	42	Maryland	142	100	42
New York	*702	286	259	Louisiana	379	265	114
New Jersey	119	43	76	Ohio	229	129	100
† Pennsylvania	124	83	41	Indiana	141	97	44
"	63	40	23				

The foreign population in 1850 was about one eighth
of the native and free negro. It would seem, then, but
natural that the convictions among the native should be
eight times as numerous as among the foreign. By an
examination of the above table, it will be seen that the
foreign convicts average, taking all the States mentioned
together, about one half of the number of the native
convicts.

These statistics and calculations clearly prove immigration to be the chief source of crime in this country.
Besides those who are convicted of crime after their
arrival here, there are many criminals transported here
by the European governments. Crime and pauperism
are both evils, injurious to the character and standing
either of a community or a government, and for both of
them we are mainly dependent upon immigration.

EFFECT OF FOREIGN PAUPERISM AND CRIME.

It has been shown in the foregoing, that in proportion
to the native and foreign population, there are ten
foreign paupers to one American, and ten foreign crimi-

* The remaining portion are unknown.
† Two Penitentiaries.

nals to one native. The inevitable conclusion is, that immigration is an evil, and that it is the principal source of crime and pauperism in this country.

In estimating the value of immigration, or the importation of foreigners, these grievous evils demand the serious reflection and mature consideration of every reflecting individual. If viewed as a business transaction—as a mere matter of dollars and cents—it must occur to every individual that the native population must bear the burden of expenses necessary to maintain these paupers, and to bring these offenders against the laws of the country to justice.

The accompanying table exhibits the cost of foreign pauperism in the several States, as shown by the census of 1850.

A Table showing the Number and Cost of Foreign Paupers in the several States.

State.	Foreign paupers.	Cost foreign paupers.	Native paupers.	State.	Foreign paupers.	Cost foreign paupers.	Native paupers.
Maine	950	$26,600	4,553	Florida	12	147	64
N. Hampshire	747	33,577	2,553	Alabama	11	531	352
Vermont	1,611	52,098	2,043	Mississippi	12	836	248
Massachusetts	9,247	229,759	6,530	Louisiana	390	27,318	183
Rhode Island	1,445	25,865	1,115	Texas	—	—	7
Connecticut	465	23,906	1,872	Tennessee	11	337	994
New York	40,580	553,918	19,275	Arkansas	8	331	97
New Jersey	576	22,407	1,816	Kentucky	155	8,431	971
Pennsylvania	5,653	113,060	5,898	Ohio	609	25,578	1,904
Delaware	128	3,274	569	Michigan	541	12,329	649
Maryland	1,903	30,333	2,591	Indiana	322	25,597	860
Virginia	185	5,513	4,933	Illinois	411	23,217	886
N. Carolina	18	559	1,913	Missouri	1,729	30,963	1,248
S. Carolina	329	8,782	1,313	Iowa	35	1,786	100
Georgia	58	1,567	978	Wisconsin	497	10,998	169
Total,	.	.	.	.	.	68,538	66,184

To these amounts must be added the cost of maintaining the county and town paupers, which are separate from the State paupers.

The money thus expended is collected by taxation; and even though the paupers may almost wholly inhabit the cities and towns, yet they are maintained at the expense of the State, the revenues of which are raised or collected by a tax, levied upon property and business. The native population bear the burden of this tax,

6

because they constitute essentially the property-holders, and the business and financial interests of the country are almost entirely owned, managed and controlled by the native-born—excepting (with due deference to the natural instincts and peculiar habits of the foreigners)—the brewing and consumption of lager-bier, root beer, and various other nauseous and disgusting liquors.

States do not tax the products of their soil ; consequently, wheat, corn, cotton, rice, sugar, and tobacco, the agricultural staples of this country, are not taxed in their natural and native condition. After they have been matured, collected, and conveyed to market, where they become articles of merchandise, subject to the rules, regulations, and pecuniary fluctuations of commerce and trade—the cotton being manufactured into articles of clothing, wheat into flour, and rice and sugar prepared for domestic and culinary purposes—then it is that the producers, the husbandman and mechanic, become consumers of these products of the soil, and of their own labor and attention. As articles of commerce and trade, they have been taxed by the State authorities, in the form of revenue and license charges, levied upon the merchants and tradesmen. These revenue and license charges constitute a part of the value of the article, or are estimated by the dealer as a part of his actual expenses, which is reimbursed to him by his profits on the articles sold ; hence it is clear that the tillers of the land bear the largest proportion of all taxes.

It must also be borne in mind that drunkenness and disease are necessary accompaniments or promoters of crime and pauperism. An examination of the jail and work-house statistics (before cited) show clearly that the largest proportion of offences against morality, good order, and decency, which are never punished by penitentiary imprisonment, are committed by foreigners ; and the expenses of maintaining these petty criminals or offenders are levied upon the county or town in which the jail, work-house, or house of refuge is located, in which these offenders are imprisoned.

These species of crime are far more deleterious to the well-being and comfort of society, and prosperity of business, than those grave offences which are punished by death, or long and solitary confinement, because they are of more frequent repetition, and are soon forgotten by the unobservant; and their constant occurrence, and the slight punishments inflicted, inure the victim to crime and immorality, and prove destructive to the moral culture and training of the young.

The following police statistics demonstrate the truth of these observations:

Statistics of Pauperism, Crime, and Destitution.

JERSEY CITY PRISON FOR 1854.

Americans, ...	44
Colored, ...	7
Foreigners	1,043

POLICE STATISTICS FOR PHILADELPHIA.

Americans	443
Foreigners	1,509

CALIFORNIA POLICE STATISTICS.

Americans	195
Foreigners	805

1855.

PHILADELPHIA—THIRD WARD.

During the year, the number of arrests made in the Third Ward amount to 3,276.

Americans	761
Colored	67
Foreigners	2,448

Of the latter, 2,166 came from Ireland !

STATISTICS OF FOURTEENTH WARD.

During the year 1855, the total arrests of this Ward foot up a total of 623.

Americans (including colored)	341
Foreigners	282

From Ireland, 198 ! In this Ward, it will be remembered, the foreign population is quite limited.

POLICE STATISTICS OF THE NINTH WARD.

Lieutenant Whittmore, of the Ninth Ward, has collated the statistics of that Ward for the year 1855, ending December 31st, 1855, from which it appears that the total of arrests amount to 1,207.

Americans	442
Colored	41
Foreigners	724

Of the latter, 644 came from Ireland!

JERSEY CITY PRISON.

Committed for the month of November	64
Americans	5
Foreigners	59
From Ireland	52

There were committed to the Jersey City Prison, during the month of December, a total of 56.

Americans (including colored)	8
Foreigners	49

From Ireland, 40.

NEWARK (N. J.) POLICE STATISTICS.

The "Newark Mercury" published a synopsis of the City Marshal' annual report, from which it appears, that during the year, the year, the total of arrests amounted to 794.

Americans	129
Colored	42
Foreigners	623

Of the latter, 533 came from Ireland!

Total Arrests for the month of November	81
Americans	16
Colored	3
Foreigners	62

From Ireland, 54!

For the month of December, the total of arrests amounted to 94.

Americans	12
Colored	7
Foreigners	75

Of the latter, 69 came from Ireland!

BOSTON POLICE REPORT FOR NOVEMBER.

Whole number arrested	1,188
Americans	219
Foreigners	969
Whole number accommodated with lodgings at the public expense for the same period	726
Americans	214
Foreigners	512

An examination of the hospital reports and statistics, exhibits too plainly the source of much of the disease which infects the large seaboard towns and cities, and which is from thence propagated throughout the surrounding country. In Philadelphia, New York, Boston, Baltimore, Norfolk, and New Orleans, which cities are heavily taxed for the support and medical care of diseased paupers, much the largest portion of the patients are *foreigners*, many of whom are transferred directly from the immigrant ships to hospitals. In the cities, those direful and pestilential diseases, ship fever, yellow fever, and small pox, are almost exclusively confined to the filthy alleys, lanes, and streets, and low, damp, filthy, and ill-ventilated haunts, which are exclusively tenanted by *foreigners.*

In corroboration of this statement it is but necessary to refer to the table below, which gives the number of patients both native and foreign admitted into the Pennsylvania Hospital, which was compiled by Mr. Sanderson, and published in his work entitled " Republican Landmarks :"

	U. States.	Ireland.	All other countries.		U. States.	Ireland.	All other countries.
1842	438	300	86	1849	648	758	246
1843	406	300	99	1850	760	812	243
1844	474	348	116	1851	626	887	353
1845	470	354	131	1852	607	783	256
1846	479	447	147	1853	618	782	307
1847	559	563	155	1854	379	902	350
1848	627	702	217				
					7,291	7,938	2,605

The aggregate number of foreigners admitted was 10,343 against 7,291 natives. By a comparison of the number admitted each year, both of native and foreign, with the native and foreign of the city of Philadelphia for each year respectively, it will be seen that the number of foreigners, in proportion to the population, far exceeds the number of native in proportion to the native population. It is needless to pursue this investigation any further; sufficient has been adduced to show the disparity between the foreign and native population, both morally and physically.

These convicts, criminals, paupers, and diseased persons, against the "insidious and destructive influences" of which Mayor Wood appealed to the President for protection, never exercised any political privilege in their native countries. They have enjoyed neither privilege nor position, and by their "long career of crime and destitution have learned no *laws either civil or political;*" and yet, the same persons are by the existing laws entitled to all the political privileges of the native born. Is it just? Is it right? Many of them have been inmates of jail, penitentiaries, and poor-houses.

From the foregoing the following are the logical deductions :

1. That immigration is the source of crime.
2. That immigration is the source of pauperism.
3. That immigration conduces to disease, disorder, and immorality.
4. It is a tax upon the property and business pursuits of the native. Besides this, they are bought up at elections, and control them, and make riot, bloodshed, and murder.

Formerly, the better class came. The old Scotch merchant and Dutch farmer were clever. They came with their substance, not only to adopt a country, but to help to build it up. But they that come *now* come to *live* upon the country.

It needs no comment. No more potent argument could be urged in favor of the present "American Reformation." Pauperism and crime are the inevitable results of foreign immigration. Yet, to gratify demagogues and unprincipled partisan politicians, must we continue, by Congressional legislation, to encourage the importation of pauperism, crime, and destitution? No national purpose can be promoted, no republican institutions can be sustained, by such a course of policy. Besides the direct result, there are many collateral influences, consequent upon the unrestricted importation of foreigners.

RELATIVE INTELLIGENCE OF THE NATIVE AND FOREIGN
POPULATION.

Now, that foreign pauperism and crime have been fully considered, it is but just and proper that a similar comparison should be instituted between the two classes of population intellectually. It is very readily shown from facts collected from De Bow's compendium of the 7th census, that the comparative educational superiority of the native far exceeds the foreign.

The native white population of the United States is 17,312,487; of these, 4.55 per cent. are uneducated, or one in every twenty-two natives; the foreign white population is 2,240,581; of these, 8.71 per cent. are uneducated, or one in twelve; thus it is readily perceived that the ratio of illiterate or uneducated among the foreign, is nearly twice as great as among the native. The accompanying table exhibits these facts:

In the New England States the per cent. of illiterate among the foreign is 14.63; whereas, among the free colored in the same States, it is but 8.45. The ignorant natives who speak our language, have been reared under free institutions, and are acquainted with the practical workings of our government; the ignorant foreigner is totally unacquainted with the language, has not enjoyed the advantages of experience and practical observation of the complex machinery of our government, and is consequently far inferior, intellectually, to the uneducated native. He cannot understand the theory of a free government, because he is destitute of the knowledge sufficient to comprehend its objects, purposes and blessings. He cannot acquaint himself with its practical operation and direct and immediate advantages to himself, because he wants the experience and observation, which *birth* and *habits* have taught; besides, he is totally unacquainted with our language, and has been reared under institutions hostile to personal liberty, to free institutions, and to a Republican government; hence

Ratio of Illiterate Persons—Foreign Native and Free Colored; also, per cent. of Native and Foreign at School, in 1850:

Geographical Divisions.	WHITES								FREE COLORED.	
	NATIVE.				FOREIGN.					
	Native, including unknown.	Illiterate.	Ratio.	Whites at school at 5 and under 15 per cent.	Foreign.	Illiterate.	Ratio.	Whites at school at 5 and under 15 per cent.	Illiterate.	Ratio per cent.
New England	2,839,651	6,219	.26	122.57	805,444	44,692	14.63	52.60	1,873	8.45
Middle States	5,219,747	96,181	1.84	—	1,079,300	108,096	9.55	—	51,111	22.42
Southern States	2,247,948	209,082	9.30	51.53	43,218	2,982	5.28	21.00	19,989	21.20
Southwestern States	1,946,468	163,788	8.41	—	104,314	9,511	9.12	—	5,018	18.54
Northwestern States	5,343,818	265,515	4.97	80.28	679,499	31,470	4.63	52.05	12,399	21.44
California and Territor's	154,855	27,099	17.50	—	28,806	4,063	14.18	—	127	12.47
Slave States	5,905,748	494,161	8.37	56.09	816,670	20,178	6.37	27.23	38,444	24.75
Free States	11,406,759	273,623	2.40	96.90	1,923,911	174,986	9.09	50.25	23,078	16.55
Total	17,812,487	787,784	4.55	82.25	2,240,581	195,114	8.71	47.00	90,522	21.08

it is, that foreigners are so prone to congregate together, to organize themselves into clubs, societies, and even communities, occupying entire sections of a county, State, and of the country. These *foreign* organizations are dangerous to our established institutions; because, wherever they have been in our country, they have repudiated the fundamental principles of our government.

So far as a knowledge of our institutions is concerned, the entire foreign population may be, and should be classed as ignorant, illiterate and uneducated; for the experience of the past, has most clearly proved that their ignorance of Republican institutions constitutes the most grievous and dangerous evil of foreign immigration. But notwithstanding the ratio of foreign illiterate is nearly double that of the native, yet the ratio of children between five and fifteen years of age, being taught in our schools bears the same relative proportion among the native and foreign. The per cent. of native white children in the schools is 82.25, of the foreign 47.00. This is a most important fact. Our schools are open to all, free to all, and in most of the States free of expense to the parent or child, yet the foreign population refuse to avail themselves of these advantages, refuse the offer of a free government, to educate their offspring. It is not only important, but alarming; it evinces the tenacity with which this class of our population adheres to the habits, customs, and superstitions which characterize foreign countries, and unfits them for the exercise of political franchises in this.

The per cent. of native illiterate, white and free negro, to the total of both native over 20 years of age, is 10.35. The per cent. of the foreign illiterate to the total foreign population over 20 years of age, is 14.51. Thus, in every phase in which we can view this question, the native population possesses superior intellectual and educational advantages to the foreign.

To show more clearly this intellectual disparity
6*

between the foreign and native population, we have constructed the following table:

	Per cent. of the entire population, illiterate.	Per cent. of those over 20 years of age, illiterate.	Per cent. of children under 15 years in schools.
Native population,	4.55	10.35	82.25
Foreign population.	8.71	14.51	47.00

In the native population, in estimating the per cent. of illiterate above 20 years of age, the free negro population is included; thus giving to the foreign population a very great advantage in the calculation; yet the native exhibits a much less per cent. of illiterate than the *foreign*. This simple table, the data for which are to be found in the census of 1850, demonstrates the fact that immigration is the source or cause of much the largest proportion of ignorance, blind and superstitious ignorance, which is spread over this land, marring the beauty of its institutions and clogging the wheels of a free government, which can only move regularly and systematically when guided by intelligent beings.

CHAPTER X.

FOREIGN IMMIGRATION.

THE immigration to this country was—

From 1790 to 1810, ...	120,000
" 1810 to 1820, ...	114,000
" 1820 to 1830, ...	203,979
" 1830 to 1840, ...	776,500
" 1840 to 1850, ...	1,542,850
" 1850 to 1856, ...	1,899,025

And statistics show that during the present decade, from 1850 to 1860, in regularly increasing ratio, nearly four millions of aliens will probably be poured in upon us.

With this alarming decennial ratio of increase—with the astonishing statistical facts that nearly four-fifths of the beggary, two-thirds of the pauperism, and more than three-fifths of the crime, spring from our foreign population; that more than half the public charities, more than half the prisons and alms-houses, more than half the police and the cost of administering criminal justice, are for foreigners—the people should demand of their statesmen, and wise statesmanship suggests, that National and State legislation should interfere to direct, ameliorate, and control these elements, so far as it may be done within the limits of the Constitution.

The calculation in the Census (see Abstract, p. 30) is, that if it increases as it has, in thirty-five years from this time, the population of this country will exceed that of France, England, Spain, Portugal, Sweden, and

Switzerland, all combined. And any one who will make the calculation will find that in fifteen years the foreign will outnumber the native population. The quantity of the immigration is therefore alarming; but the quality is still more so.

In 1854, the number of foreign immigrants was 460,474, of which 307,639 arrived at the port of New York. The white population of North Carolina is only a little over 500,000, so that nearly enough came to settle a State as populous as North Carolina in one year.

The following table exhibits the white population of the States therein enumerated, and the excess of foreign immigrants to this country, during the year 1854, above the respective populations of the several States; or, in other words, it demonstrates the alarming fact that the foreign immigration of 1854 was more than sufficient to settle a State as populous as any therein mentioned. The third column, headed, the "ratio of foreign immigration to the population," shows the number of States, equal in white population to the State mentioned, which might have been settled by the immigration of one single year, 1854:

A TABLE COMPARING THE WHITE POPULATION OF THE STATES THEREIN ENUMERATED WITH THE FOREIGN IMMIGRATION OF 1854, AND SHOWING THE EXCESS OF FOREIGN IMMIGRANTS FOR THIS YEAR ABOVE THE RESPECTIVE POPULATION OF THE SEVERAL STATES.

State.	White population.	Excess of immigration.	Ratio of, &c.	State.	White population.	Excess of immigration.	Ratio of, &c
Arkansas,	162,189	298,285	2.85	Maryland,	417,943	42,531	1
Alabama,	426,514	33,960	1	Michigan,	395,071	65,403	1
California,	91,635	368,839	4	Mississippi,	295,718	164,756	1.55
South Carolina,	274,563	185,911	1.67	N. Hampshire,	317,456	143,648	1.50
Connecticut,	363,099	93,375	1	Rhode Island,	143,875	316,699	3
Delaware,	71,169	389,305	6	Texas,	154,034	306,440	3
Florida,	47,203	413,271	10	Vermont,	213,402	247,072	2
Iowa,	191,881	268,593	2	Wisconsin,	304,756	155,718	1.55
Louisiana,	225,491	234,981	2				

Analyze this table. The last Congress passed an act for the organization of the Territories of Kansas and

Nebraska, in which it granted the *elective franchise* to every immigrant, who might settle in either of said Territories. If this principle, thus established by the National Government, is hereafter to become the organic law of future States, the subjects and serfs of European despots will soon exercise an absolute control over the Federal Legislature. As soon as the Territories acquire the requisite population, they have a right to apply for admission into the Union, upon an equal footing with other States. By reference to the foregoing table, it will be seen that the foreign immigration of 1854 was sufficient to have settled nearly three States equal in white population to Arkansas, two equal to Iowa, three equal to Texas, four to California, three to Rhode Island, six to Delaware, or ten to Florida; so that under the principle of the Kansas-Nebraska law, while immigrants continue to come at the rate of 1854, there may be within one year ten new States applying for admission into the Union, entitled to their twenty senators in the U. S. Senate; and yet, this would be but the senatorial representation of 460,474 foreigners. These ten States would be equal each in white population, to the State of Florida, each one of which would be entitled to a representative in the House of Representatives, and two senators. If the ratio of immigration continues to 1860 as it has been since 1850, during the years from 1850 to 1860 there will have come four millions of foreigners, enough to settle one hundred States equal in white population to Florida, thirty equal to Rhode Island, sixteen equal to Louisiana, Iowa, Arkansas, South Carolina, or Vermont, or eight equal either to Alabama, Connecticut, Maryland, Michigan, Mississippi, New Hampshire, or Wisconsin, or forty equal to California. So that it is within the range of possibility for the senatorial representation of foreigners to reach two hundred senators and one hundred representatives. The Senate is now composed of but sixty-two senators, representing thirty-one States. Is not this a most startling revelation? Is it not time to heed the warning voice of the immortal Washington?

> " Against the insidious wiles of foreign influence—I conjure you to believe me, fellow-citizens—the jealousy of a free people ought to be constantly awake; since history and experience prove that foreign influence is one of the most baneful foes of a republican government."

Thus spoke the Father of his country, and has not the "future" arrived, to which the sagacious Jefferson referred, when he said

> " I hope we may find some means, in future, of shielding ourselves from foreign influence, political, commercial, or in whatever form it may be attempted. I can scarcely withhold myself from joining in the wish of Silas Dean, ' that there were an ocean of fire between this and the old world.' "

Truly, indeed, have the prophetic words of Washington been fulfilled—"*foreign influence is one of the most baneful foes of a republican government.*"

The question will naturally occur to every reader, is there sufficient territorial area which may thus be settled by *foreigners?* The present territorial area is 1,723,821 square miles, or 1,103,245,440 acres of land, which is sufficient to form forty-six States equal in size to either Kentucky or Maine. Adopting either as the basis, one representing the slave States, the other the free States, the danger to the settled and established institutions of either class of States is apparent to every reflecting mind; and, judging from the present ratio of *foreign* immigration, who is there who will deny that these dangers may not overwhelm us during the present decennial period?

The density of the population of the United States in 1850 was 7.90 persons per square mile. The immigration of 1854 would settle at this ratio of density, sixty-four thousand square miles.

The following table exhibits the number of square

miles of the States enumerated, as compared with the
number of square miles which, at the density of the
population of the United States, would be settled by the
immigration of 1854, also, the present representation
of each in the House of Representatives, and the
number of representatives to which the immigration of
1854 would be entitled according to the representatives
of the States respectively.

States.	Sq. miles.	Sq. miles settled by immigration of 1854.	Representation.	Representation of immigration of 1854 according to the States.	States.	Sq. miles.	Sq. miles settled by immigration of 1854.	Representation.	Representation of immigration of 1854 according to the States.
Alabama,	50,722	64,000	7	9	Maryland,	11,124	64,000	6	34
Arkansas,	52,198	64,000	2	3	Massachusetts,	7,800	64,000	11	88
Connecticut,	4,674	64,000	4	52	N. Hampshire,	9,280	64,000	3	21
Delaware,	2,120	64,000	1	44	N. Jersey,	8,320	64,000	5	38
Kentucky,	37,680	64,000	10	15	R. Island,	1,306	64,000	2	96
Maine,	31,766	64,000	7	14					

Thus it is seen that at the rate of density of the population of the United States, the immigration of 1854
will settle sixty-four thousand square miles, which,
according to the representation by square miles of the
States respectively, would entitle the immigration of
1854 to the number of representatives under that head,
(in Congress) opposite the States respectively in the
above table. But this is a matter more of curiosity
than of any practical bearing, under existing laws, upon
the legislation of the country, because representation in
the popular branch of Congress is in proportion to the
population, and not to the square mile.

The comparison, to be properly instituted between
the States and the immigration of 1854, should be based
upon the density of the population of each State
respectively, and the number of square miles which the
immigration of 1854 would settle at the rate of density
of the population of the States respectively, thus:

States.	Square miles.	Density of population.	No. of square miles which the immigration of 1854 would settle at the ratio of density of the State.	Representation of the State.	Representation of the immigration of 1854 at that ratio.
Arkansas, . . .	53,198	4.02	114,297	2	4
California,. . .	155,980	.59	780,464	2	8
Florida, . . .	59,268	1.48	311,131	1	5
Iowa, . . .	50,914	3.78	121,808	2	5
Michigan, . . .	56,243	7.07	65,120	4	4,
Texas, . . .	237,504	0.89	516,261	2	5
Wisconsin. . .	53,924	5.66	81,373	3	5

By this table it is shown that the immigration of 1854 would settle an area of territory as densely as Arkansas, which would make two States equal in area to the State of Arkansas, and consequently be entitled to four representatives in Congress, it would likewise make four equal to California, and be entitled to eight representatives, two and a half equal to Iowa, and be entitled to five representatives, and so on.

Again, the immigration of 1854 is greater than the aggregate of the population of Rhode Island and Wisconsin, which two States have five representatives in Congress. The effect of immigration upon the national legislature may be further exemplified by dividing the immigration of 1854 by the ratio of representation; it will give five as the number of representatives, and if the aggregate of the immigration for the years 51, 52, 53, 54, which is 1,581,276, be taken, it will give 17 as the number of representatives due to immigration, were a new apportionment now made.

The density of the population in any of the States enumerated in the last table is far greater than it is in any of the territories of the United States, and the immigration of 1854, properly distributed, is sufficient to give to each and all of the seven organized territories the requisite population to entitle them to admission into the Union as States, and in each territory a majority of the population would be foreigners, thus the immigration of one single year would be entitled to seven representatives in the House of Representatives, and fourteen senators, and in that event the number of States under the absolute control of foreigners would constitute 5.42 of the whole number of States ; and the immigration of the past five years is sufficient to give the requisite population to entitle them to State organizations, to eighteen territories, exclusive of the native population which may emigrate to the same. These are practical illustrations of the political power of foreigners, based upon positive data.

The exercise or abuse of the elective franchise, are not the only political evils incident to immigration ; these may be corrected by the enactment of stringent laws, but so long as immigration is permitted, the population increases by virtue thereof, and in the apportionment of Federal Representatives to the States, the foreign population enters into the calculation, consequently great injustice may be done to certain localities or sections of the country. Political power and ascendency may be thus transferred from one section to another, and the equilibrium between the various interests of the several sections be thus destroyed. The immigrant population is becoming every day more disposed to settle in certain parts of the country, and even, if they should not be permitted to vote, they would augment the political power and influence of that particular section of the country by adding to its Federal representation. To avoid this evil, immigration must be arrested, or only the native population must be considered in apportioning Federal representation to the States ; but even in the latter case, the influence of foreigners would not be gotten rid of, because it would be exerted through the native children of foreigners. The only means, then, which can be adopted to get rid entirely of all these evils, social, moral, physical, and political, is to arrest immigration.

CHAPTER XI.

UNDER this head it is proposed to consider the power now possessed and exercised by the foreign population in the popular elections of the country.

In 1850, there were 2,240,581 white foreigners in this country ; of which there were—

Natives of Ireland	961,719	Natives of Germany	573,225
Natives of England	278,675	Natives of British America	147,700
Natives of Scotland	70,550	Natives of France	54,069
Natives of Wales	29,868	Natives of all other countries	95,022

The foreign is 11.46 per cent of the whole free population of this country. Since 1850, foreign immigration has vastly increased ; but in all the tables which follow, the calculations, estimates, and results, are based upon the above data, which are to be found in the census of 1850, and which, even though they do not reach the present political power of the foreign population, demonstrate sufficient to startle even the most skeptical.

The following table shows the popular vote of the States at the last Presidential election ; the foreign population and foreign vote of each State in 1850 ; and the relative proportion of the foreign to the native vote. It will be perceived that the comparison is too liberal to the foreign population, because its political power of 1850 is compared with the popular vote of 1852, when the foreign vote must have been much stronger than two years previous.

One-seventh is the natural proportion of voters in any population; but among the foreign population of this country, the proportion is much greater, because the proportion of females and children to the males is much less than among the native population. The Census statistics of 1850 clearly exhibit this fact. Among the native white population, there are forty-nine females in a hundred; among the foreign population there are but forty-four. The ratio of children to the native and foreign population, respectively, is much greater; hence the proportion of one-sixth has been adopted.

A TABLE SHOWING THE POPULAR AND FOREIGN VOTE, FOREIGN POPU-
LATION OF EACH STATE, AND THE RELATIVE PROPORTION OF THE
FOREIGN AND NATIVE VOTE.

States.				Popular vote in 1852.	Foreign pop. in 1850.	Foreign vote in 1850.	Prop. of foreign. votes to native For. Nat.		
Maine	.	.	.	81,182	31,695	5,282	1	to	14
N. Hampshire	.	.	.	52,839	14,527	2,376	1	to	21
Vermont	.	.	.	43,839	33,688	5.614	1	to	7
Mass.	.	.	.	132,936	163,598	27.266	1	to	3½
Rhode Island	.	.	.	16,005	23,832	3,972	1	to	8
Connecticut	.	.	.	66,768	38.374	6,562	1	to	9
* New York	.	.	.	522,294	655,224	109,204	1	to	3½
New Jersey	.	.	.	83.221	59.814	9,802	1	to	7
Pennsylvania	.	.	.	486,216	303,300	50,550	1	to	8½
Delaware	.	.	.	12 672	5,243	874	1	to	13
Maryland	.	.	.	75,153	51,000	8.502	1	to	8
Virginia	.	.	.	129.545	22.953	4,825	1	to	26
North Carolina	.	.	.	78,861	2,565	427	1	to	184
Georgia	.	.	.	51,365	6,452	1,075	1	to	46
Florida	.	.	.	7.193	2.740	456	1	to	14
Alabama	.	.	.	41,919	7,492	1,248	1	to	32
Mississippi	.	.	.	43.424	4.782	797	1	to	53
Louisiana	.	.	.	35.902	67,308	11,218	1	to	2 1-6
Texas	.	.	.	18,547	17,620	2 936	1	to	5
Tennessee	.	.	.	115.916	5,638	949	1	to	121
Kentucky	.	.	.	111,139	31,401	5,233	1	to	22
Ohio	.	.	.	353.429	218,099	36.349	1	to	6
Michigan	.	.	.	82,939	54.593	9,097	1	to	8
Indiana	.	.	.	183,134	55,537	9,256	1	to	18
Illinois	.	.	.	145,497	111,890	18,660	1	to	6
Missouri	.	.	.	65,586	76.570	12.761	1	to	4
Iowa	.	.	.	16,847	20.968	3,494	1	to	4
Wisconsin	.	.	.	64.712	110,471	18.411	1	to	2½
California	.	.	.	74.736	21,628	10,000	1	to	6
Arkansas	.	.	.	19,574	1,468	244	1	to	90

By the above table, it is shown, that in Iowa and Missouri, one-fourth of the voters are persons of foreign

* The Census recently taken gives foreign votes 135,676.

birth; in Rhode Island, Massachusetts, and New York, one-third; in Wisconsin and Louisiana, about one-half; in Texas, one-fifth; in California, Illinois and Ohio, one-sixth; in Michigan, Maryland, Pennsylvania, and Connecticut, from one-eighth to one-ninth, and in Vermont and New Jersey, one-seventh. In these fifteen States, the foreign vote constitutes a very formidable *political power*. In all the remaining States it is sufficiently potent to be felt in closely-contested elections. Missouri, Texas, Louisiana, and Maryland are Southern States; the others, Northern; and yet, notwithstanding the difference in their domestic institutions, they suffer equally from this foreign influence. In view of these *facts*, and the impending danger from this *foreign political influence*, is it not important that the present naturalization laws should either be amended or repealed? Should not this influence, which Washington declared to be " *one of the most baneful foes of a republican government*," be arrested? The period has surely arrived.

This table demonstrates one other fact. All the territorial possessions lie in the west, northwest or southwest. In these three directions the tide of immigration is rapidly tending. It will be observed that the border States, Louisiana, Texas, Arkansas, Missouri, Wisconsin, Illinois, Michigan, and Ohio, are most seriously affected by this foreign influence; and the inference is clear and indisputable, that all the territorial possessions will be settled by foreigners. These results are not merely conjectural. The facts and evidences are before you, and it needs but little foresight and political sagacity to anticipate a result so dangerous to republican institutions.

Again, during the year 1854, there were 460,474 immigrants. Five out of every nine foreigners are males, and five out of every seven of these males are adults; consequently, there were 255,805 males, of which 182,720 were adults. Under the present laws, and the laxity of their execution, how easy it is to manufacture these adults into voters. In one single year the immi-

grant adult population exceeded that of any State in the
Union, excepting New York, Pennsylvania, and Ohio.
The immigrant male adults who arrived in 1850 were (if
they have availed themselves of the privileges of the existing laws), entitled to vote in 1855, and those who arrived
in 1851 will be entitled to vote during the present year,
so that the popular vote of each year has been increased
by the addition of an average of one hundred thousand
foreign votes for the past five years.

There is one other idea which may be considered in
this connection. The fifth article of the Constitution of
the United States, provides that the Constitution shall
not be amended, unless the amendment is proposed by
two-thirds of both Houses of Congress, " or on the application of the legislatures of two-thirds of the several
States," which amendment must be "ratified by the
legislatures of three-fourths of the several States, or by
conventions in three-fourths thereof." May it not be
possible—indeed, it is highly probable—that when, in
the course of events, the foreign population, now pouring in from Europe, shall have obtained the numerical
strength which has been shown may soon occur, this
very constitutional provision may be seized hold of,
and through it some odious and oppressive feature may
be engrafted upon the Constitution bequeathed to us by
our forefathers ? What that feature may be, no living
being can tell. It may be that slavery will be interdic-
ted or freedom suppressed. It may be the union of
CHURCH AND STATE, and that Church may be the Catholic or the Protestant, the Mormon or German infidelity.
It may be that some despot will sway over this broad
and free land, under the authority of suffrage, as Santa
Anna and Louis Napoleon have done in their respective
countries. Let us ponder on these reflections, these
probabilities of the future. Is there no remedy ? Have
we already reached the "slough of Despond," and for-
gottten the warning of the great and good Washington ?
Let us retreat from this yawning gulf we have approached

too near. The danger is imminent, pēril is certain. In what direction shall we beat our retreat? The horde of *foreign immigrants* is pressing upon us. Shall we close the portals of entrance? or shall we curtail their political powers and privileges? " Self-preservation is the first law of nature." Justice to ourselves and to posterity demands some enactment, by which the impending danger may be averted, the institutions of the country preserved intact, and the liberty for which the patriots of the revolution fought and bled, perpetuated.

In the foregoing estimate of the foreign vote, the greatest liberality has been shown; but one-sixth of the entire foreign population in a State has been set down as voters, whereas five-ninths of the adult foreign population might, with more justice to the subject, have been estimated as the proportion of foreign vote to the foreign population; if such had been adopted as the rule in making the calculations, the number of foreign votes would have far exceeded the number at which it has been estimated.

FOREIGN VOTERS IN THE CITIES.

Certain presses throughout the country, have asserted and re-asserted that the foreign vote is so small, that its influence could not be felt in any election. An examination of the following statistics, plainly exhibits the controlling influence of the foreign votes in the cities named. The proportion of votes in the two classes is based upon the established rule—that one-seventh of the population are voters. This is true with regard to the native population. Among the immigrant population, as has been previous stated, the relative proportion of females and children to the males, is much less than among the native population; consequently, the proportion of voters among the foreigners is much greater than one-seventh; but this rule has been adhered to in the following table, so as to allow the foreign population every advantage in the calculation:

	Native population.	Native vote.	Foreign population.	Foreign vote.
Albany	31,162	4,452	16,591	2,370
Baltimore	130,491	18,642	35,492	5,070
Boston *	88,498	12,642	46,677	6,668
Chicago	13,693	1,956	15,782	2,240
Cincinnati	68,558	9,937	54,541	7,793
Detroit	11,055	1,579	9,923	1,417
Louisville	25,079	3,582	12.461	1,780
Milwaukie	7,181	1,026	42,782	6,111
Mobile	9,565	1,366	4,086	583
New Orleans . . .	50,470	7,210	48,601	6,943
New York	277,752	39,822	235,733	33,090
Philadelphia . . .	286,346	40,906	121,699	17,371
St. Louis	36,529	5,218	38,397	5,485

In Chicago, St. Louis, and Milwaukie, the foreign vote exceeds the native; in New Orleans, Detroit, New York, and Cincinnati, they are nearly equal; in the remaining cities, the foreign vote is about one-half of the native. In any one of these cities, the foreign vote is sufficiently powerful to decide the contest between either of the old political organizations.

By this it will be seen that not only may aliens control the local elections, and thus secure themselves a large part of the corporation patronage, but, by impressing themselves upon the State elections, secure to themselves an undue influence upon the Federal Government. With this astounding proportion which the alien bears to the native population, it is not surprising that the watchmen, police officers, and other subordinate officers, should be filled chiefly with men who have too recently arrived in the country to comprehend or to care for its interests. Let us, therefore, limit this power of political action on the part of the aliens, and our people will be more contented, and our institutions more permanent.

During the year 1854, 307,639 foreigners arrived in the city of New York. According to the usual rule,

---

* A recent census of this city, gives a total foreign population of 86,886, and the native 76,293.

one-seventh of these will in five years be voters. At the expiration of five years, provided the existing naturalization laws be strictly enforced, the voting population of that city will be increased forty-four thousand. Even now, its native vote exceeds the foreign vote only 6,000. It is true, many may not remain in the city of New York, and well it may be so, or else the city would, of necessity, be under the absolute control of persons unacquainted with its institutions and their management.

The following statistics in relation to the city of New York, are copied from the " N. Y. Express " of a recent date :

ALIENS IN NEW YORK CITIES.

The State census discloses the following facts, as the number of aliens in the cities of the State :

Albany	13,344	New York	. . .	232,678
Auburn	1,461	Utica	. . .	5,825
Hudson	841	Syracuse	. . .	6,192
Poughkeepsie	2,164	Oswego	. . .	4,144
Buffalo	26,086	Troy	. . .	8,736
Brooklyn	62,105	Schenectady	. .	1,653
Rochester	12,701			
Total			. . .	377,930

CURIOUS CITY STATISTICS.

The inequality of the Senatorial districts in New York city is remarkable. This table excludes aliens and people of color not taxed.

Third district—Mr. Sickles	50,581
Fourth district—Mr. Petty	87,600
Fifth district—Mr. Spencer	64,846
Sixth District—Mr. Brooks	83,348

The aliens in the above districts, who are not included in the above enumerations, are—

3d district	41,468	5th district	30,404
4th district	58,016	6th district	102,790

Mr. Brooks thus represents 183,349—but 29,629 less than his colleagues. In the same (6th) district, the number of—

Native voters are	19,817
Naturalized	18,596
Excess of native over foreign vote . . .	1,321

If the laws remain as at present, immigration will increase, and the annual increase of foreign voters will at least reach half the number before stated. Is it not time, then, that some steps should be taken to rescue the city from the impending danger? The city of New York is not alone. Most of the seaboard towns are suffering from the same cause. It is true, Congressional liberality, or rather demagogism, has enticed many to the uncultivated wilds of the West, and the evils of foreignism have been thus extended and diffused. Several of the new States are now completely under the control of foreigners; and, unless further legislation is had, curtailing their elective privileges, we venture the prediction that every State hereafter admitted into the Union will be absolutely under the control of the foreign voters.

THE INFLUENCE OF FOREIGN VOTERS IN THE LAST PRESIDENTIAL ELECTION.

The following table shows that the popular majority for Pierce over Scott falls far short of the foreign vote. Thus:

Pierce's vote, ...	1,602,663
Scott's vote, ...	1,385,990
Pierce's majority, ...	216,673
Foreign vote, ...	367,320
Pierce's majority, ...	216,673
	150,647

The foreign vote exceeded Pierce's majority over Scott, 150,647 votes.

But there is another view which may be taken of this election. It is contended that the foreign vote is so scattered over the country that its effect is not perceptible, at any particular point. The following tabular statement of the election in 1852 for President, shows that the foreign vote in the States mentioned exceed the majorities given to General Pierce.

7

States.	Foreign population.	Foreign vote.	Pierce's majority.	Electoral vote for Pierce.
New York, . .	655,224	93,317	27,201	35
Pennsylvania, .	303,105	43,300	19,446	27
Maryland, . .	51,011	7,287	4,945	8
Louisiana, . .	67,308	9,615	1,392	6
Missouri, . .	76,570	10,938	7,698	9
Illinois, . .	111,860	15,980	15,653	11
Ohio, . .	218,099	31,157	16,694	23
Wisconsin, . .	110,471	15,781	11,418	5
Iowa, . .	20,968	2,995	1,180	4
Rhode Island, .	23,832	3,404	1,109	4
Connecticut, .	38,374	5,482	2,890	6
Delaware, . .	5,243	749	25	3
New Jersey, .	59,804	8,543	5,749	7
California, . .	21,628	10,000	5,694	4
		258,543	120,094	152

It is thus demonstrated that in *each* of these fourteen States the *foreign* vote was *larger* than the majority given for General Pierce; and it is also demonstrated that the aggregate foreign vote of these fourteen States is *more than twice* the whole number of the aggregate of General Pierce's majorities in said States. If even *one-half* of the foreign vote had been given to General Scott, he would have been elected instead of General Pierce!

In North Carolina, too, the foreign vote was 366, and General Pierce's majority but 686; so that if Scott instead of Pierce had received this foreign vote, he would have received the electoral vote of North Carolina by a majority of 146 votes!

The time is not far distant when even Virginia, by the increase of *foreign* voters, will be under *their* influence and control, if the contests in that State continue to be carried on between the former rival parties.

These simple calculations demonstrate clearly that the foreign vote is sufficiently powerful to decide the contest between any two political parties, which has heretofore divided the native citizens of this country, and from the existence of that fact has grown many of the abuses, and much of the corruption which are calculated to bring discredit upon the nation, and to effect-nally destroy that great safeguard of American liberty—the ballot-box.

The equality of the two former great political parties has given to the foreign vote additional power, because each, aiming at success, have bid for the foreign vote, and in too many instances purchased it at the sacrifice of principle and of American nationality. The election of 1852 is a fair illustration, but equally fairly and clearly would prior elections exhibit the strength of, and the power wielded by our foreign born population in the elections of the country. The success of either of the former political parties depended upon the foreign vote, and upon whichever side that was cast, success resulted thereto; and this circumstance demonstrates the vacillating character of the foreigners, at one time voting with one party, and at another with the other, thus holding out to each an inducement to pander to their caprices, and to shoulder their absurdities. They held the balance of power and exercised that power for their own aggrandizement.

The same investigation might be made in reference to the elections of 1844 and 1848, with a similar result, but this and previous tables contain all the information necessary to convince any one, who is not hopelessly blind to the truth, that the government of the United States will, unless the influence of foreigners be curtailed, be ultimately overwhelmed with it.

A VIEW OF FOREIGN INFLUENCE IN THE HOUSE OF REPRESENTATIVES.

The present ratio of representation in the House of Representatives is 93,423. The following table exhibits the foreign population of the States therein named, in 1850, and the number of Representatives in Congress due to this foreign population.

State	Foreign population	No. Representatives	State	Foreign population	No. Representatives
Massachusetts . .	163,598	1	Illinois	111,860	1
New York . . .	665,224	7	Wisconsin . . .	110,471	1
Pennsylvania . .	303,300	3			—
Ohio	218,099	2			15

This is the actual and undeniable representation of the foreign population in the popular branches of the National Legislature.

The number of Representatives due to the foreign population in the States above mentioned has been obtained by dividing the foreign population of the States respectively by the representative ratio (93,433). But there are thirteen members assigned, under the late law apportioning the representatives, to those States having the largest residuary fraction, over and above the ratio of representation.

In nine of the thirteen States which were entitled to an additional representative, in consequence of the residuary fraction, the foreign population exceeds the " *residuary fraction*," viz. : Massachusetts, Rhode Island, Connecticut, Pennsylvania, Maryland, Kentucky, Missouri, Indiana, and Louisiana—consequently, according to the census of 1850, the representation due to the foreign population in the House of Representatives is as follows :

Massachusetts	.	.	2	Rhode Island	.	.	.	1
New York	.	.	7	Connecticut	.	.	.	1
Pennsylvania	.	.	4	Kentucky	.	.	.	1
Ohio	.	.	2	Missouri	.	.	.	1
Illinois	.	.	1	Indiana	.	.	.	1
Wisconsin	.	.	1	Louisiana	.	.	.	1
Maryland	.	.	1					—
								24

These statistics show that the foreign representation in the popular branch of Congress is twenty-four members, twenty coming from the free States and four from the Southern States. We have obtained this number (twenty-four) by examining carefully the statistics of each State, and relative proportion of its foreign and native population; but if we take the aggregate foreign population, 2,240,581, and divide it by the ratio of representation (93,423), we obtain precisely the same number, twenty-four.

Thus it is clear that the *foreign* representation in the United States House of Representatives amounts to this number, and certainly it will not now be contended that *foreignism* is not sufficiently powerful in this country to impress itself upon the legislation of the country. Indeed, scarcely a session of Congress has passed, within the last five years, that one-third of the time has not been wasted in legislating exclusively for the foreigner, each member vying with the others in his generosity to this class of population.

SHOULD THE SOUTH FEAR IMMIGRATION ?

The entire foreign population in 1850, was 2,240,581, of which 378,204 resided in the Southern States, which would give, under the existing law regulating representation, four representatives to the Southern and twenty to the Northern or free States. This simple calculation demonstrates that the representative preponderance of the free States is owing to immigration. The present Federal representation of the Northern States is 144 members, and of the South 90, which gives to the North 54 majority. If the representation due the foreign immigration of the North be deducted from its present representation and added to that of the South, the North would have 124 members and the South 110, or if the representation due to the foreign population be deducted from each, the North would have 120 members and the South 86, a majority of 34 in favor of the North, whereas now the majority is 54, showing a gain to the South of 20 members.

The fears of the South from the North consist in the rapid advancement of the latter in political power, and this political power is increased annually by immigration from Europe, and in the rapidity of increase of the foreign over the native population.

Besides the political power, the South has other dangers to apprehend from other evils. By a table (before cited) published in the compendium of the seventh census, giving the number of convicts in prisons and penitentiaries of the several States, out of every ten thousand of the population, the proportion of natives and foreigners to that number is as follows :

	Foreign.		Native.			Foreign.		Native.
In Maine	5	to	1		In Vermont . . .	8	to	1
In Kentucky . . .	6	to	1		In South Carolina .	28	to	1
In Mississippi . . .	5	to	1		In Alabama . . .	50	to	1
In New York . . .	3	to	1		In Georgia	6	to	1
In Tennessee . . .	15	to	2		In Indiana	4	to	1

The relative proportion of foreign crime to native in the States of Kentucky, Tennessee, South Carolina, and Alabama, is far greater than that among any of the Northern States, and in Georgia and Mississippi it is equal to any of the Northern States.

In Georgia, Kentucky, Tennessee, Mississippi, Alabama, and South Carolina, the aggregate foreign population in 1850 was 64,079, of whom, in every ten thousand, the average proportion of convicts was 30.43, whereas in every ten thousand of natives, the average proportion was but 1.65.

The proportion of convicts in the various prisons and penitentiaries, on 30th June, 1850, native white, foreign and negro, in every ten thousand of the native white, foreign and negro population, in the Northern and Southern States, stands thus :

	Native White.	Foreign.	Negro.
Southern States . . .	1.673	11.684	.938
Northern States . . .	1.991	5.868	28.743

And the total proportion of the foreign of the North and the South is three times as great as that of the negro in both sections. It is clearly deducible from these facts that the South has most to fear from immigration. Besides the physical and political power which immigration gives to the North, of which the South has so long complained, the South suffers comparatively more from the accompanying evils of immigration, crime and pauperism, than the North.

-----◆◆◆-----

CHAPTER XII.

FOREIGNERS IN GOVERNMENT EMPLOY.

It is impossible to determine positively the relative proportion of foreigners in government employ, because the nativities of all the employés are not to be ascertained. The " Blue Book "—" a register of the officers and agents, civil, military, and naval in the service of the United States," is the only authority upon which any calculation can be based. This register is published biennially by the government, the last was issued in the fall of 1855, and contains all the data upon which the following table has been constructed.

The nativities of 4084 are reported, of which 607 are of foreign birth. The nativities of the Post Masters and Superintendents of Light houses are not reported. The following table comprises the civil and diplomatic appointments of the State department, the employees in the War Department, the employés in the Treasury and Interior Departments at Washington, and all the employés of which the nativities were given, in the other branches of the General Government mentioned. The Mints, Light houses, and Coast Survey, properly belonging to the Treasury Department, as do the Indian Pension and Patent Offices to the Interior, but they have been arranged, as in the table, for convenience merely. In the Navy Department at Washington all the civil employes are American born.

How Employed.	Natives.	Foreigners.	Proportion. F. N.	Salary of Foreig's.
State Department	24	5	1 to 5	7,400.00
Ministers Abroad	25	3	1 " 8	13,500.00
Consuls	160	42	1 " 4	40,000.00
Commercial Agents	9	8	1 " 1	8,000.00
Treasury Department	330	35	1 " 9	42,500.00
Coast Survey	43	35	1 " 1	37,880.00
United States Mints	55	6	1 " 9	12,000.00
Keepers of Light houses . . .	374	55	1 " 7	22,870.00
Custom Houses	1,908	305	1 " 6	280,380.82
Department Interior	19	4	1 " 5	2,593.00
Patent Office	66	5	1 " 10	5,000.00
General Land Office	347	32	1 " 15	35,156.00
Indian Office	144	18	1 " 9	15,600.00
Pension Office	182	12	1 " 15	15,640.00
Commr. of Pub. Buildings . . .	30	23	1 " 1	13,020.00
War Department	71	19	1 " 4	20,760.00
Total	3,477	607	1 " 5.77	567,300.42

According to the statistics in the offices above named, 14.86 per. cent of the employés are foreigners, more than one-sixth, to whom is paid annually out of the Treasury, $567,300.42.

In the New York custom-house there are employed 107 foreigners; in the Philadelphia, 27; Baltimore, 11; New Orleans, 54, and in San Francisco, 23. In Iowa there are but three surveyors of customs, and two are foreigners. In Indiana three, and two foreigners. In the custom-house at Chicago there are seven foreign employés, and two American born. At Milwaukie there are six foreign and three American employés, a Norwegian, two Germans, and three Irishmen, and three Americans. The average salary of the foreigners is $685.20, of the natives but $560. At Chicago the average salary of the foreigners is $804.04; of the Americans but $480. In the United States Coast Survey the average yearly pay of the natives is $713; of the foreigners $1,082. These are the relative salaries of the natives and foreigners employed in the office at Washington, as taken from the pay-roll for July, 1855. In this office, Charles A. Schott and Thomas W. Werner, both foreigners, receive an average of $1,456 per annum, while Eugene Nutly, an American, for performing similar duty, receives $1,200. George McCoy and

A. Rolle, foreigners, receive, as engravers, an average of $1,850 per annum, while John Knight and F. Dankworth, American engravers, receive but $1,700. Four of the assistants are foreigners; two receive $2,500 per annum, one $1,600, and one $1,500. One of these assistants is not naturalized, and probably two of them.

In the office of weights and measures there are but four Americans, and seven foreigners. In this office the standard weights and measures of the United States are manufactured, and it will hardly be contended that there are no American mechanics competent to manufacture the American standard weights and measures.

The foreign population is 11.46 per cent. of the whole white population of the United States. The foreign office-holders is 14,86 per cent of the whole number of office-holders. Again, the foreign population is about one-eleventh of the whole population, yet the foreign office-holders are nearly one-sixth of the whole number of office-holders. If the offices were distributed in due proportion to the two classes of population, native and foreign, the foreigners should only have one-eleventh of the whole number. Out of 4,084, the foreigners should have but 378, whereas they have 607,129 above their due proportion. These facts may be cited as additional proof of the disposition of the immigrant population to acquire and to hold on to political power, and not only political power, but to feed upon the government. Besides the immense amount expended in this country to maintain foreign paupers, to prosecute foreign criminals, and to import foreigners, the additional sum of $567,300 is paid out of the treasury of the United States in the shape of salaries to foreigners, and in several instances foreigners are the disbursing agents of the government.

Americans are certainly entitled to a pro rata share of the honors and of the offices, yet so powerful is the influence of the foreign population, that this pro rata share has not been allotted to them. The foreigners enjoy the excess. If such discrimination is to be exercised against the "American born," is it not natural that they who, it must be admitted, have the prior right to the honors and offices, will hasten that conflict of races, which, whenever it comes, will deluge the land in blood? America should be ruled by America.

CHAPTER XIII.

UNCONSTITUTIONAL FOR STATES TO NATURALIZE ALIENS.

This subject is one of the highest importance. Prior to the adoption of the Federal Constitution, the States possessed and exercised the power of granting naturalization. The consequence of it was, that there were various and discordant rules adopted. Even since, several of the States have, by provisions in their constitutions, admitted aliens to the right of citizenship, upon a residence of six months, and a simple declaration of an intention of becoming a citizen. Such provisions, in any of the State constitutions, are clearly in violation of the Constitution of the United States. An alien, to become a citizen of the United States, must have resided within its limits five years, and taken the oath of allegiance, and no one can be a citizen of any one of the States without being a citizen of the United States; if it be otherwise, there must necessarily be two classes of citizens within the United States, viz.: State citizens, and United States citizens. Again, if a State can naturalize an alien, it can confer citizenship upon a person who is not a citizen of the United States. Hence, a person might be enjoying all the privileges of a citizen within a State, entitled to the elective franchise, and to the protection of its laws, and possessing the right to vote for members of Congress, President of the United

States, and for members of the State legislature, which elects the senators of the United States, and yet not be a citizen of the United States. The Constitution provides, that members of the House of Representatives shall be elected in the same manner as the members of the popular branch of the State legislature are elected. If a State can naturalize or confer the elective franchise upon an alien, and grant him the privilege of voting for the members of the popular branch of her legislature, she, at the same time, grants him the privilege of voting for a member of the House of Representatives, and yet he is not a citizen of the United States.

The following extract from an address, written by Mr. Vespasian Ellis, editor of the " *American Organ*," clearly sets forth the unconstitutionality of naturalization by a State.

" Mr. Madison, in page 202 of the "Federalist," advocating the adoption of the Federal Constitution, says :

" ' In one State, residence for a short time confers all the rights of citizenship; in another, qualifications of greater importance are required. An alien, therefore, legally incapacitated for certain rights in the latter, may, by previous residence only, in the former, elude his incapacity; and thus the law of one State be preposterously rendered paramount to the law of another, within the jurisdiction of the other.'

" This was the condition of things whilst the different States exercised the power of naturalization. The evils of it are manifest. Another writer (Rawle on the Constitution, page 85), after describing the evils of these conflicting provisions, adds,

" ' The evil could not be better remedied than by vesting the exclusive power in Congress.'

" The provisions of the Constitution on this subject are in the following words. In article I., section 9, it reads—

" ' Congress shall have power to establish a uniform rule of naturalization.'

" In article I., section 9, it reads—

" ' The migration or importation of such persons as any of the States now existing shall think proper to admit, shall not be prohibited by the Congress, prior to the year 1808.'

" In article IV., section 2, it reads—

" ' The citizens of each State shall be entitled to the privileges and immunities of citizens in the several States."

" These are all the provisions of the Constitution affecting this question. By the first clause cited above, the general power is granted to establish a uniform rule. By the second clause cited, the power of prohibiting immigration is conferred. The suppression of the slave-trade was, no doubt, particularly aimed at in this clause; but the term ' migration, or importation of such persons,' &c., cannot be confined to any specific class of persons. They are general and comprehensive terms; and, there being no ambiguity of expression, they must be construed to mean what they plainly import. The third clause cited, makes the citizens of each State citizens of the whole United States. Under those three clauses, it seems plain that the most ample authority is conferred upon Congress to regulate the whole question of immigration exclusively. Congress may establish the rule, change the rule, abrogate the rule, and prohibit foreign immigration entirely. The power, whilst exercised by the States, produced the evils of conflicting legislation, and contradictory rules. That evil was to be remedied. It was remedied by transferring the power to the national legislature, where it most properly belongs. Is not, then, this power in Congress exclusive? Rawle so considers it, in his treatise before cited, page 85. Bayard so considers it, in his view of the Constitution, page 71. He says:

" 'This power is, from its nature, exclusive ; for, if the several States could legislate on this subject, they might require very different qualifications for citizens, and aliens would become citizens of the United States upon very unequal terms, according to the laws of the particular States in which they might be naturalized.'

" It was held in the Circuit Court of the United States, at Philadelphia, in 1792, in the case of Collet vs. Collet, 2 Dallas, 294, that the State governments had concurrent authority with Congress, upon the subject of naturalization. But this decision has been overruled. In the Circuit Court, in 1854, Judge Washington decided in the case of Golden vs. Prince, 3 Washington's Circuit Reports, 314, that this power was exclusive in Congress. And at a later period in the case of Chirac vs. Chirac, 2 Wheaton, page 269, Chief Justice Marshall said, that, 'It certainly ought not to be controverted; that the power of naturalization was vested exclusively in Congress.' In the case of Houston vs. Moore, 5 Wheaton, page 49, Justice Story, alluding to this power, considers it exclusive, on the ground of there being a direct repugnancy or incompatibility in the exercise of it by the States.

" In the very able commentaries of this same judge, upon the Constitution of the United States, vol. 3, chap. 16, sec. 538, he uses the following language : ' It follows from the very nature of this power, that to be useful, it must be exclusive; for a concurrent power in the States would bring back all the evils and embarrassments which the uniform rule of the Constitution was designed to remedy. And accordingly, though there was a momentary hesitation when the Constitution first went into operation, whether the power might not still be exercised by the States, subject only to the control of Congress, so far as the legislation of the latter extended, as the supreme law, yet it is now firmly established to be exclusive in Congress.'

" Chancellor Kent, in commenting upon this subject, and reviewing the authorities, does not hesitate to say that ' the weight of authority, as well as of reason, may therefore be considered in favor of this construction.' If, then, the opinions of Bayard, Rawle, Story, and Kent, sanctioned by the decisions of the circuit and Supreme Courts of the United States, are to be regarded as authority, the position is impregnable, and the question clear beyond all controversy, that Congress has the exclusive power of legislation on the important subject of naturalization. Indeed, if it were otherwise, what would prevent New York, or any other State, from naturalizing a million of Africans, who, ipso facto, would be ' entitled to all the privileges and immunities of citizens in the several States,' under the 2d section of the 4th article of the Constitution? Justice, reason, and authority, forbid such a construction as this. If it should still be insisted, however, that because the Supreme Court has decided that the power of Congress to pass a uniform bankrupt law is not exclusive, but that, in the absence of a law of Congress, a State may pass insolvent or bankrupt laws, and that forasmuch as the power of Congress over this subject is conferred in the same clause with the power to establish a uniform rule of naturalization, therefore the same principle of construction should apply ; it may be answered, that the effect of the exercise of the two powers by individual States, would be totally different. We have seen that if the several States could naturalize foreigners, whilst the clause of the Constitution conferring upon the citizens of each State all the immunities of citizens of the several States, is unrepealed, it would be in the power of any one State to confer upon foreigners the right to be citizens of all the other States. But the insolvent or bankrupt laws of an individual State could only operate within its limits. It has been decided repeatedly, that ' the discharge of an insolvent under a State law will not discharge a debt due to a citizen of another State who does not make himself a party to the proceeding under the law.' See 2d vol. Kent's Com., page 392, and the cases there cited. It may also be observed, that whilst the power over the subject of naturalization was conferred upon Congress to remedy an evil which would again prevail under the construction that this power in Congress is not exclusive, the power to establish an uniform bankrupt law was not conferred to remedy any particular existing evil, but granted to enable Congress to effect a positive good, whilst the failure of Congress to exercise the latter power would not result in any particular general mischief. For these reasons, doubtless, the same courts and the same jurists have held the one power to be exclusive and the other not so. We repeat, then, that the power of Congress over the subject of naturalizing foreigners is general, comprehensive, and exclusive. The individual States, therefore, cannot pass laws of naturalization, for they have surrendered this power to Congress, and it may be exercised or not, in the discretion of that body. If exercised, therefore, it would seem also to be indisputable, that Congress may impose whatever conditions, limitations, and restrictions it may please in reference to the time, mode and terms of naturalization."

During the discussion of the bill to admit Michigan into the Union, in the constitution of which was a clause allowing aliens to vote, Mr. Calhoun said :

"The Constitution confers on Congress the authority to pass uniform laws of naturalization. This will not be questioned; nor will it be, that the effect of naturalization is to remove alienage.

"To remove alienage, is simply to put the foreigner in the condition of a native born. To this extent the act of naturalization goes, and no further.   *   *

"The next position is no less certain, that when Congress has exercised its authority by passing a uniform law of naturalization (as it has) it excludes the right of exercising a similar authority on the part of the State. To suppose that the States *could pass naturalization* acts of their own, after Congress had passed an uniform law of naturalization, would be to make the provision of the Constitution nugatory.   *   *

"I have shown that a citizen is not an alien, and that alienage is an unsuperable barrier, till removed to citizenship; and that it can only be removed by complying with the act of Congress. It follows, of course, that a State cannot, of its own authority, make an alien a citizen without such compliance.   *   *   *

"Whatever difference of opinion there may be as to what other rights appertain to a citizen, all must, at least, agree that he has the right to petition, and also to claim the protection of his government. These belong to him as a member of the body politic, and the possession of them is what separates citizens of the lowest condition from aliens and slaves. To suppose that a State can make an alien a citizen of the State, or, to present the question more specifically, can confer on him the right of voting, would involve the absurdity of giving him a direct and immediate control over the action of the General Government, from which he has no right to claim the protection, and to which he has no right to present a petition. That the full force of the absurdity may be felt, it must be borne in mind, that every department of the General Government is either directly or indirectly under the control of the voters in the several States. The Constitution wisely provides that the voters for the most numerous branch of the Legislatures in the several States, shall vote for the members of the House of Representatives; and as the members of this body (Senate) are chosen by the Legislatures of the States, and the Presidential electors either by the Legislature, or votes in the several States, as I have stated, that the action of the General Government, is either directly or indirectly under the control of the voters in the several States. Now, admit that a State may confer the right of voting on all aliens, and it will follow as a necessary consequence, that we might have among our constituents, persons who have not the right to claim the protection of the government, or to present a petition to it.   *   *   *

"But a still greater difficulty remains. Suppose a war should be declared between the United States, and the country to which the alien belongs; suppose for instance, that South Carolina should confer the right of voting on alien subjects of Great Britain residing within her limits, and that war should be declared between the two countries; what, in such an event, would be the condition of that portion of our voters? They, as alien enemies would be liable to be seized under the laws of Congress, and to have their goods confiscated and themselves imprisoned, or sent out of the country. The principle that leads to such consequences cannot be true; and I venture nothing in asserting that Carolina, at least, will never assent to incorporate, as members of her body politic, those who might be placed in so degraded a condition, and so completely under the control of the General Government.

"But let me pass from these (as it appears to me conclusive) and inquire what were the objects of the Constitution, in conferring on Congress the authority of passing uniform laws of naturalization; from which, if I mistake not, arguments not less conclusive may be drawn in support of the position for which I contend.

"In conferring this power, the framers of the Constitution must have had two objects in view: one to prevent competition between the States, in holding out inducements for the immigration of foreigners; and the other to prevent their improper influence over the General Government, through such States as might naturalize foreigners, and, could confer on them the right of exercising the elective franchise before they could be sufficiently informed of the nature of our institutions, or were interested in their preservation. Both of these objects would be defeated if the States may confer on aliens the right of voting, and the other privileges belonging to citizens."

In answer to the argument urged by his colleague, Mr. Preston, that the constitutions of Vermont, North Carolina and Rhode Island, permitted aliens to vote, Mr. Calhoun said:

" It is sufficient answer to say, that their constitutions were adopted before the existence of the General Government, and that the provisions which permitted aliens to vote, constituted a portion of their constitutions, when they came into the Union. North Carolina has since amended hers, and limited the right of voting to citizens. If Vermont and Rhode Island have not done the same, it most be attributed to that *vis inertia* which indisposes most States to alter their constitutions, or to accidental omission. But we have the authority of the Senator from North Carolina, (Mr. Mangum,) and also the Senator from Vermont, (Mr. Prentiss,) that under the decisions of the courts, of the respective States, their constitutions have been so constructed, since they entered the Union, as to confine the right of voting and holding lands to citizens of the States, so as to conform to the principle for which I contend. To cite a case in point, my colleague ought to show that under the constitution of any State, formed since the adoption of the Constitution of the Union, the right of voting has been conferred on an alien. There is not, I believe, an example of the kind ; * from which I infer the deep and universal conviction which has pervaded the public mind, that a State has no authority to confer such a right."

In answer to a question put by Mr. Preston, Mr. Calhoun said:

" My colleague cites the example of Louisiana, which was admitted into the Union, without requiring the inhabitants, at the time, to conform to the act of naturalization. I must think the instance not in point. That was a case of the incorporation of a foreign community, which had been acquired by treaty, as a member of our confederacy. At the time of the acquisition, they were subjects of France, and owed their allegiance to that government. The treaty transferred their allegiance to the United States ; and the difficulty of incorporating Louisiana into the Union, arose, not under the naturalization, but the right of acquiring foreign possessions by purchase, and the right of incorporating such possession into the Union. These were felt at the time to be questions of great difficulty. Mr. Jefferson himself, under whose administration the purchase was made, doubted the right, and suggested the necessity of an alteration of the Constitution to meet the case ; and if the example of the admission is now to be used to establish the principle, that a State may confer citizenship on an alien, we may all live to regret that the Constitution was not amended according to the suggestion.
" My colleague insists, that, to deny the right for which he contends, would be to confer on Congress the right of prescribing who should or should not be entitled to vote in the State, and exercise the other privileges belonging to citizens ; and portrayed in strong language, the danger to the rights of the States from such authority. If his views are correct in this respect, the danger would, indeed, be imminent ; but I cannot concur in their correctness. Under the view which I have taken, the authority of

* Since then Illinois, Wisconsin and Indiana have adopted such provisions in their constitutions.

Congress is limited to the simple point of passing uniform laws of naturalization; or, as I have shown, simply to remove alienage. To this extent, it may clearly go, under the Constitution; and it is no less clear that it cannot go an inch beyond, without palpably transcending its powers and violating the Constitution. Every other privilege except those which necessarily flow from the removal of alienage, must be conferred by the Constitution and the authority of the State."

In speaking directly in reference to the bill he said:

"This bill prescribes that the *people* of Michigan who shall vote for the convention to form her constitution, on becoming a State, * * * I ask who are the people of Michigan? Taken in the ordinary sense, it means every body, of every age, of every sex, of every complexion, white, black, or red, aliens as well as citizens. Regarded in this light, to pass this bill would sanction the principle that Congress *may authorize an* alien to vote, or confer that high privilege on the run-away slaves from Kentucky, Virginia, or elsewhere, and thus elevate them to the condition of citizens, enjoying under the Constitution, all the rights and privileges in the States of the Union, which appertain to citizenship. * * * * * *

"If it be meant by the people of Michigan, the qualified voters under her incipient constitution, * * * then are we sanctioning the right of aliens to vote. Michigan has attempted to confer this right on that portion of her inhabitants. She has no authority to confer such right under the Constitution. I have conclusively shown that a State does not possess it, much less a territory which possesses no power, except such as is conferred by Congress. Congress has conferred no such power on Michigan, nor, indeed, could confer it, as it has no authority, under the Constitution, over the subject, except to pass *uniform laws of naturalization.*"

In a speech delivered by Senator Clayton, upon the amendment submitted by him * to strike out of the Kansas Nebraska bill, that clause which granted the elective franchise to aliens within the territories of Kansas and Nebraska, he said:

"Citizen and alien have been properly considered as correlative terms. A citizen is not an alien, and an alien is not a citizen. A citizen may be defined to be any person residing in any State or territory of the United States, who enjoys all the rights, privileges, and immunities of a man of full age, born and resident in those States or territories. What is naturalization? It is sufficient for my purpose to define it as that process, by which the Congress of the United States *removes the disabilities of alienage.* Now, what are the disabilities of alienage? In the first place, an alien cannot vote unless the power is specially conferred on him. In the next place, an alien is not entitled to, and cannot demand protection from the government. He is under no obligations to it, and may make war upon it, without incurring the penalties of treason. He cannot petition the government for any wrong which he has suffered. If he be here while the country from which he came is at war with the United States, he is liable, under an act of Congress, to be ordered out of the country within a given time, and therefore he has no right of permanent residence here in such a contingency as that which I have mentioned. These are all known and acknowledged disabilities of alienage. The disqualification of an alien to vote does not merely arise from an act of Congress, or an act of a State Legislature. It exists as an incident to alienage here and everywhere. It must be removed by competent authority, and by positive enactment, before an alien can exercise the rights of suffrage. It is inherent in the very nature of alienage, that it cannot exercise a right by which it may govern others.

* Known as the "Clayton amendment."

There can be no just ideas of popular rights and national sovereignty, or national independence when the notion prevails that an alien ought to vote. Give this right to foreigners, as is proposed by this bill, and you surrender all that distinguishes him from an American. Nay, you give these rights to strangers, with whom you may be at war to-morrow, while you refuse to your own citizens in one State, the right to vote in another. For by the law of nearly every State in this Union, some qualification is required for a voter besides naturalization, and generally, among others, residence for a stated period is an indispensable pre-requisite. But, by the provisions of this bill, any alien may vote in these territories without previous residence, or paying a cent of tax to support the government, which he is to control by his vote.

"Now, sir, naturalization being nothing more nor less than the removal of the disabilities of alienage, Congress can pass a law for that purpose, provided it be 'uniform,' either for the removal of the whole of these disabilities in one law, or for the removal of any one, two, or three, or any other number, in separate bills or laws. That inference flows irresistibly from the previous position. Congress, therefore has the power, under the Constitution of the United States, to provide, that aliens may vote in all the States and territories, subject in the State to such restrictions as a State may impose, in the exercise of its reserved powers, on all voters. That would be naturalization *pro tanto*, that is, to that extent, it would remove the disability of alienage, and would be constitutional, because it would be uniform.

"Further, Congress can grant the right of petition, or any other of the rights of citizenship. It may grant them altogether, or it may, as I have said, grant them separately, always taking care that the grant is uniform; but Congress cannot grant one of these constituent parts which may make up the agregate of all the attributes or rights of citizenship to one State, and refuse it to another. It cannot, by a direct law, allow an alien to vote in Virginia, and deny him the right to vote in Delaware. If this does follow, as I clearly think it does, then I undertake to say that Congress cannot grant exemption from any disability in Nebraska, and refuse it in the other territories, and in the States of the Union, without violating that clause in the Constitution of the Union which declares that Congress shall have power to make 'uniform' laws of naturalization. A law removing all the disabilities of alienage, and thus making them citizens in Nebraska, and yet not extending that provision to the other territories and States, would be, I suppose, by everybody admitted, to be unconstitutional. Then, is it not a fair and irresistible consequence, that if Congress only remove a part of the disabilities of alienage, or if it proceed but partially or *pro tanto*, to naturalize the aliens in Nebraska, without extending the same privilege to other sections of the United States, it is decidedly and clearly unconstitutional?"

The amendment of Senator Clayton to the Kansas Nebraska Bill, provided, in effect, that in Kansas and Nebraska "the right of suffrage and holding office shall be only exercised by citizens of the United States," which was adopted by the following vote:

Yeas.—Messrs. Adams, Atchison, Badger, Bell, Benjamin, Brodhead, Brown, Butler, Clay, Clayton, Dawson, Dixon, Evans, Fitzpatrick, Houston, Hunter, Johnson, Jones, of Tennessee, Mason, Morton, Pratt, Sebastian, and Sledell—23.

Nays.—Messrs. Chase, Dodge of Wisconsin, Dodge of Iowa, Douglass, Fessenden, Fish, Foote, Gwinn, Hamlin, Jones of Iowa, Norris, Pettit, Seward, Shields,

Smith, Stuart, Summer, Toucey, Wade, Walker, and Williams—21.

The unconstitutionality of granting the elective franchise to aliens was thus affirmed by the Senate of the United States.

This same question, subsequently, came before the Senate in precisely the same form, upon the motion of Senator Pearce, of Maryland, who moved to strike from the bill which had passed the House of Representatives, to organize these territories, the same words which were included in the " Clayton Amendment." Upon this motion, Senator Brown, of Mississippi, said :

" If the section passes as it stands, it is, beyond all question, that foreigners in the territory, and not being in the service of the United States, may vote, no difference what may have been their character abroad, or what their inducement to come here—however discreditable to the country from which they came, they have nothing to do but to make a declaration of their intentions to become a citizen, and take an oath to support the Constitution, to entitle them to vote; while American citizens, who have been so from their birth, and whose characters are above reproach, if they are in the military service of their country, in the territories, will by the same act, be denied the right to vote. * * * * * * * *

" The officers commanding your army, the soldiers who are serving under your banner and who are placed upon your frontier to defend your women and children from the tomahawk of the savage, will *be denied the elective franchise*, while thousands and tens of thousands who are pouring upon our shores from every part of God's habitable globe, will be entitled to that sacred privilege. * * If Santa Anna should be expelled from Mexico tomorrow, as he may be, and should take up his residence in one of these territories, he may vote the day after he gets there, if this bill passes; and Winfield Scott, whose name is emblazoned on every page of his country's history; and whose impress is on every battle-field from the St. Lawrence to the city of Mexico, if he was there stationed at the order of the President, would not be allowed the same privilege. * * * * * * *

" I have heard before of putting foreigners on equal footing with Americans, but this is the first time when I have been called upon to give them an advantage. * *

" I cannot reconcile it to my sense of right to vote for a proposition which gives to a foreigner, and I care not who he may be, or under what circumstances he may come to our shores, the right to vote in these territories."

Senator Benjamin said :

" The Amendment now before the Senate, offered by the Senator from Maryland, commends itself to my deliberate judgment. I voted for it before."

Senator Bayard of Delaware said :

" The moment you admit the right of citizens of another country, or those who are not citizens of ours, to assume equal political rights with our own citizens, you take a long step in the progress of *denationalization*. * * Do you not *denationalize* your country when you enact that, because the man who has come here to-day declares that he means to become a citizen, he shall exercise the same political rights and privileges as if he were a citizen. * * * * * * *

" I consider the principle of this amendment absolutely necessary for the permanence of the institutions of this country, and therefore I can record my vote for no bill which authorizes a right of voting to others than citizens of the United States."

The bill finally passed with the alien clause retained in it, and aliens now exercise the elective franchise in these two territories.

THE END.

3